Best Web Sites for Kids

Trevor Meers

Contributing Writer:
Valle Dwight

Cover Illustration:
Dave Garbot

Publications International, Ltd.

Trevor Meers is an editor and columnist whose Web site reviews and articles about the Internet, the World Wide Web, and online activities appear in various computer magazines and newspapers.

Valle Dwight is an experienced computer and Internet editor, writer, and reporter. She is a contributing editor at *Family PC* magazine, a national monthly that covers computer topics for families. Valle's work has also appeared in other leading publications, including *Newsweek's E-Life*.

Cover Illustration: Dave Garbot

Louis Weber, CEO
Publications International, Ltd.
7373 North Cicero Avenue
Lincolnwood, Illinois 60712

Permission is never granted for commercial purposes.

Manufactured in China.

8 7 6 5 4 3 2 1

ISBN: 0-7853-4159-5

Contents

INTRODUCTION
What is the Internet?

Learning about the Internet starts with one symbolic step: looking around a room.

A typical kid's room would probably have some books sitting on a shelf. Maybe there's a TV in the corner. There might even be a video game system and cable stations hooked to the TV. The stereo sits quietly, waiting for someone to listen. A poster of a famous sports hero or popular musician might be hanging on one wall; maybe on another, there's a picture that some-body painted.

Next, look out the window. You're likely to see some animals, such as squirrels and birds. Maybe a car is cruising past, or an adult is mowing the lawn. Perhaps some kids are playing at a nearby park. A mailbox stands by the street, a street that leads out of the neighborhood and into the rest of the world.

Now come back inside. Take a look at the computer. Every-thing you've just seen in the room and outside the house is also in the computer, as long as the computer is connected to the World Wide Web (and the electrical socket). The Internet lets a computer connect to millions of other computers all around the planet. That means that kids can sit at their desks and read stories, watch videos, look at pictures, play video games, learn about animals, talk to other kids, and visit just about any place they can think of. Using the Internet is like having a special ship that can travel anywhere. It even lets kids travel through time to learn about the past!

There's really no limit to what kids can find "online" (that's another word for using the Web). Even the experts who are busy developing the Internet don't know how far this cyber-world can go!

Any kid can use the Web, because the controls are really easy to learn. To go online, users just have to point to pictures and buttons on the screen and click on them with the computer's mouse or track ball. Some Web sites get a little more complicated, but the people who run these sites are usually good about explaining any new skills that kids need to learn.

When kids use the Web, their computers get information from other computers all over the world. They talk to each other over the same telephone lines people use when they have conversations on the phone. That's why if you only have one phone line, nobody in the house can make a phone call while someone else is using the Web. Parents can set up the computer to make calls by hooking up a modem. Once the computer starts talking to other computers, kids can take over and start visiting Web sites. (Some parents might have a separate phone line put in just for the computer.)

Users decide which Web site to look at just like they decide which TV channel to watch. However, while a TV might have only about ten channels, and TVs hooked up to cable or a satellite dish can be tuned into anywhere from 30 to hundreds of channels, a computer has access to somewhere in the neighborhood of *200 million* Web sites!

Kids tell the computer which Web site they want to look at by typing in an address like this: "http://www.nick.com." This tells the computer to call the Nickelodeon computer and bring up its Web page. A lot of times visitors simply click buttons to change sites instead of taking the time to look up and type in a new Web page addresses.

With so many Web sites to choose from, it's hard to decide where to visit. That's where we come in. *Best Web Sites for Kids* is just that: a list of a bunch of cool sites for kids to check out. We've done most of the research and work, so that kids will have a head start on their Web activities. Look through the book for stuff that sounds cool, then start exploring.

It's time to get busy and explore the world, and all it has to offer, through your computer! However, before you get started, read on for a discussion of a few important safety tips.

Kids learn to look both ways before crossing a street. They know not to talk to strangers around town. But many kids may not know the safety rules for the Internet. Surfing the Web without knowing how to be safe is as dumb as crossing a highway while wearing a blindfold!

All kinds of people use the Internet. There are millions of nice people using the Net for all kinds of great things, such as those listed in this book. But there are also some tricky and immoral people using the Internet, and some of them want to scare kids or even hurt them if they get a chance. Anyone can avoid the creeps and have a great time on the Web if they observe these simple guidelines:

- Kids should follow their parents' rules about when to go online and what kinds of things to do there.

- Kids shouldn't give their full names, ages, phone numbers, or street and e-mail addresses or passwords to *anyone* until they've asked their parents.

- Nobody should put their picture online without asking their parents for permission.

- Sometimes people online say they'd like to meet in person. No way! Kids should never agree to meet anyone in person until their parents say it's OK and agree to go along to the meeting.

- The Internet lets people hide what they really look like, so it's easy for weirdos to lie about who they are. Smart kids don't believe what everyone says online.

- Surfing the Web should be a family activity so that Mom and Dad can sometimes see what kinds of things kids do online (and kids can see how their parents use the Web).

- If anyone online ever says something on a Web page, in e-mail, or in a chat room that makes a kid uncomfortable, the kid should leave immediately and quit talking to them. Then, the kid should tell their parents what happened. Kids should never feel like it's their fault when someone else says something bad.

- Some programs have "viruses" in them. These viruses can make a computer sick, just like some viruses make people sick. Whenever users download a program from a Web site, they should use special anti-virus software to scan files and make sure they're safe.

On the next page is a picture of a Web browser. These programs have the tools that help guide kids around the Web.

Location bar: This is where users tell a computer what Web page they want to view. Typing in a Web address tells the computer what Web page to dial up.

Link: Text that appears on the computer screen in a different color and underlined (called a hypertext link) helps kids reach other Web pages. By pointing to it with their mouse arrow, the arrow turns to a pointing finger and users can click on the words to visit another Web page.

Buttons: Click these buttons to visit a different Web page. The words explain what page the button will jump to. Buttons function in the same way as links.

Back button: This button brings the user back to the previous Web page viewed. Clicking the Back button is like flipping backward through the pages of a book.

Forward button: Once a user has used the back button, they can also use the Forward button. While clicking the Back button brings up pages the user has seen before, clicking the Forward button flips ahead again through the pages.

Scroll bar: Clicking the arrow on this bar moves a Web page up or down. When the whole page doesn't fit in the window, click the arrow at the bottom to display more of the page.

Print button: Click this button to print the Web page on paper. Kids should make sure that it is legal to print a specific page or

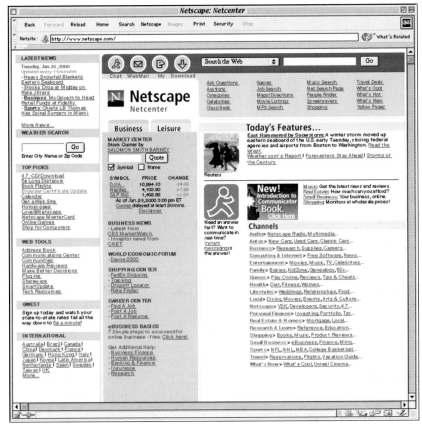

A Web page looks tricky at first, but soon you'll have it figured out.

pages from a Web site before doing so. Web page designers usually make it clear if it *isn't* all right.

Favorites: This feature, sometimes called Bookmarks, makes it easy for people to visit their favorite Web sites. When users pull up this feature, they see a list of Web sites. They can click the sites' names to go see them. This saves users from having to type in a Web page's address every time they want to visit. Users can usually add a site they're looking at to this list by opening Favorites, then clicking Add To Favorites.

Chapter 1

By Kids, For Kids

When something important is built, it's usually done by adults. But on the Web, kids get their chance. Almost anybody can build a Web page with a little practice, so lots of kids build Web sites that are as good as (or better than) those created by adults. Plus, a lot of sites created by adults invite kids to send in contributions, such as stories and pictures. The sites in this section show off what kids are putting online.

Some kids go all out trying to help other kids on their sites. B. J. Pinchbeck is a good example. This hardworking kid lists all his favorite sites that help kids with their homework. Some kids do their hard work away from the computer. Visitors can learn about them at the Youth Hall of Fame, which recognizes kids who serve their communities or put together great ideas that work.

Many of the sites in this section aren't built to *provide* help; they are *looking* for help. In this way, kids can be a part of the Web by sending in their artwork or stories. Their material will be posted on the Web, making each of them a famous Web artist!

0)oin this club by sending in your writing

The Young Writers Club

http://www.cs.bilkent.edu.tr/~david/derya/ywc.html

Any kid who likes to write stories, poems, or anything else will dig The Young Writers Club, where any visitor can become one of the people writing the Web site. This is a kid's big chance to get started as a writer.

The Writers Club wants kids to send in as much writing as they can. There's even a Member of the Year award given in January and July to the kid who sends in the most material. The club suggests ideas to help young authors get started by asking them to describe their scariest moments or to explain why certain songs are their favorites.

It's OK to just read what other kids say, too. The Club includes plenty of stories, book and movie reviews, opinions about topics such as the Internet, and more. Check out the Global Wave magazine, which is written by kids. Special tips even help writers build their own Web pages.

Since this is a club, visitors get the chance to hang out with new friends. They can make "keypals" (online pen pals) and talk in chat sessions. Kids team up with each other to write a continuing story where everybody gets to add their ideas and make the story go wherever their imaginations want it to.

A guide to sites for kids—by kids like you

B. J. Pinchbeck's Homework Helper

http://www.bjpinchbeck.com/

Nobody knows better what a drag homework can be than a kid. Why not turn to another kid for help on getting homework done? B. J. Pinchbeck helps students find the information

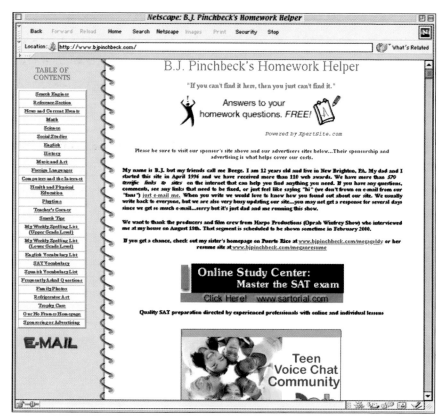

Kids know how hard homework is. Ask one for help!

they need to finish homework for any school subject. Students don't have to poke around the Internet for information, because B. J. tells everyone exactly where to look for everything from simple dictionaries to online art galleries. His site has links to nearly 600 great sites, and it's always growing.

On the main site page, the left side of the screen shows all kinds of school subjects. Click one such as Math, Science, or Social Studies for a list of sites that can help in that area. B. J. tells a little about each site so users know whether or not it sounds like something they would want to visit.

A rotating "New" button, which looks like a coin in a Nintendo game, shows the new sites in the list, so it's easy to spot what's been added since your last visit. When someone in B. J.'s family really likes a site, he lets everyone know that, too.

B. J. also knows that there is more to life than homework. The Playtime category on the left side of the screen suggests links to sites where kids can have some fun when it's time for a break from the books.

Kids sound off on videos and software

KIDS FIRST! Community

http://www.cqcm.org/kidsfirst/categf.htm

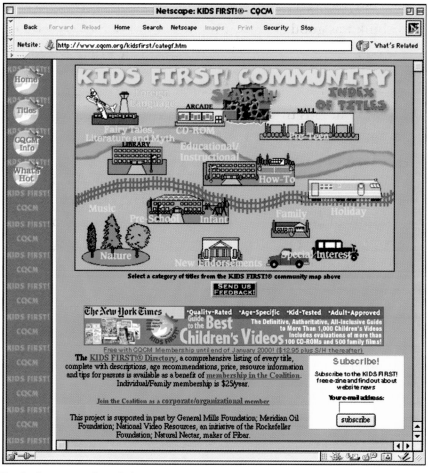

Here's where to go to hear the kid scoop on videos and games!

Who knows what kids like best? Kids! The KIDS FIRST! site knows that, so it lets kids be the reviewers and write about their favorite videos and CD-ROM computer programs. This is the place for kids to go to hear what everyone is talking about.

The kid reviewers look at videos and software that parents have picked as being kid-friendly (because they don't have violence or bad language). The kids write reviews that include what they think was good and bad about each product. Visitors start by clicking a category like CD-ROM or Fairy Tales, Literature, and Myth from the site's map. In the product reviews, the line that reads "KIDS FIRST! KID JURORS SAY" shows where users can read what kids think of the title. They'll say what is good (and not so good) about the product.

The site's Search button makes it easy to look up a specific video or program. It's a great tool for finding out what the kid jurors think of favorite products or for getting ideas about what to see next. Typing in "Pikachu," for example, brings up reviews of products with that character.

LINKS:
Family Care Foundation, Sidewalk Productions

Read stories from prize-winning kid authors

Reading Rainbow

http://gpn.unl.edu/rainbow

There's lots to see, read, and play under this Rainbow. The Reading Rainbow is famous for introducing kids to some entertaining stories, and for turning them on to reading at the same time. The Rainbow's Young Writers and Illustrators Contest lets kids get into stories in a firsthand way—by writing and illustrating their own!

The contest is run annually, and thousands of kids enter. You can check out the current winners from kindergarten through third grade. Each story is brightly illustrated, and the best part is that you can hear the young authors reading their own stories.

> The stories at this site show how well kids can write. There are amazing stories hiding inside every kid's head just waiting to be told. Kids can take a look at these tales and might get inspired to write their own stories.

These kid authors may inspire other aspiring Dav Pilkeys and Judy Blumes to get *their* words published.

In the Your Stories section, you can read even more kid-written stories. This is where the stories that have been entered in the contest appear. If you submit work, look for your name in lights right here. While in past years the entries were judged just by the story, the contest will now include judging on the illustrations, too.

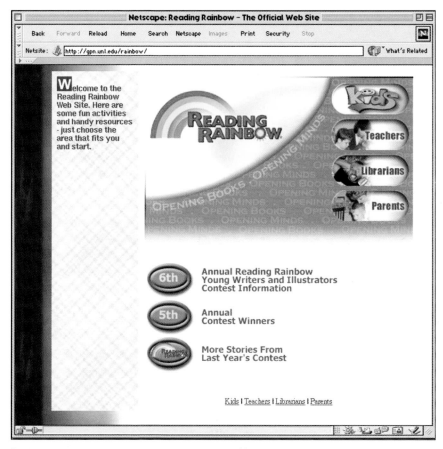

Read stories, write your own, and send in your artwork!

Elsewhere on the site, kids can play games and complete activities associated with that day's Reading Rainbow show. In the Games section, kids test their knowledge about books they've heard about on Reading Rainbow, and each day two new activities to do on and off the computer are featured.

LINKS:
Kids, Teachers, Librarians, Parents

Young stars show how helping others makes you feel great

GreatKids Network

http://www.greatkids.com

See how kids are changing the world.

What makes a GreatKid? Being great takes a lot of special qualities, but the biggest one is knowing this: Doing nice things for other people makes us feel good about ourselves.

That's the whole idea behind the GreatKids Network, a site dedicated to honoring kids who go out of their way to help others. The kids described in the GreatKids stories show others that they, too, can make a difference with a little work. The young folks here are real examples to other kids.

The Stars section tells all about different GreatKids. Jamie, for example, started food drives to help hungry people when she was nine. Now she's helped hundreds of hungry people and has become a star in newspapers and on TV—all because she wanted to help other people! Eric started using his amazing musical talent to teach other kids music when he was in seventh grade. Now, thanks to Eric, whole crowds of kids play instruments.

Other GreatKids clean up neighborhoods, write mystery stories, and invent machines. Anybody who works to do great things can be part of the GreatKids network. A special Speak Up section lets kids write in about things they've done for others lately that made them feel good.

Kids sound off in their own newspaper

Little Planet Times Kids' Newspaper

http://littleplanettimes.com

Extra! Extra! Read all about it! Kids from all over get a chance to read the news and weigh in with their opinions. In this newspaper, kids read about the residents of Little Planet and their ongoing controversies, from whether to tear down a hill to a reported sighting of a rare Bug-o-saur.

Kids start out by reading the latest edition of the *Little Planet Times* to see what issues the residents are struggling with. Once they've boned up on the news, kids can write letters to the editor with their thoughts on the local dilemma. All of the kids' opinions and ideas are published and incorporated into the news.

> In the Creative Corner, aspiring writers and artists are invited to publish their works. Read poems, stories, and even movie reviews submitted by kids from around the world. If you've got a story to tell, write it down and see it published in this worldwide newspaper.

Like any good newspaper, the *Little Planet Times* has other sections, including reviews of popular movies, songs, and books. All of these sections feature the same theme so that kids can think about the issues from a number of points of view. The Sports page has another story about the athletes of Little Planet, and kids are welcome to write in with their own news and opinions.

The topics change a few times a year, and you can always go back and see old issues. Some of the topics include stories on perseverance, friends, courage, and conflict resolution.

LINKS:
Parents & Teachers, School Spotlight, Letters

News and opinion about a special place.

An online gallery specializing in kids' art

Global Children's Art Gallery

http://www.naturalchild.com/gallery/

A lot of parents hang pictures their kids create on the family refrigerator. But it would take a gigantic refrigerator to hold pictures drawn by kids from all over the world. Since nobody has a fridge that big, there are Web sites like the Global Children's Art Gallery. It's the place where all kinds of kids can hang their pictures for the world to see. The gallery shows work from kids all over the world and even displays the flags of their countries.

Hundreds of drawings are displayed here from kids living in countries such as Korea, Canada, Australia, and even right here in the United States. The Art Gallery lists the name of each picture. Some are funny, like "Pregnant Seal and Funny Man" or "Green Fingers." Some picture names are adventurous, like the dinosaur picture called "Belosy-reptor" by a creative kid from South Korea. Kids can click any picture to see a bigger version of it. Anybody who likes one of the pictures can use the Print button on the screen to print it out.

Of course, a lot of young Web users can probably draw as well as these kids. The Global Children's Art Gallery would love to make new drawings part of the show. Any kid 12 or under can send in a picture to go on the Web site.

Come see what other kids are writing and drawing

Cyberkids Kidzeen

http://www.cyberkids.com

On this site, you can see all sorts of different creative works from kids 7 to 12 years old in the Creative Works section. And the artists? Any kid—and that means you! If you've got a great idea for a story, picture, puzzle, poem, news article, or song, you can send it in to Cyberkids and maybe it'll be posted for everyone else to see or hear.

When you click on Fun & Games, you can choose from a variety of animated stories, games, and brain-teasing puzzles. If you want to know what's going on in music, film, and books, go to the Cyberviews section and read interviews with interesting people in the arts—like "Party of Five" star Lacey Chabert, for example.

There are also some great resources on this site. The Launchpad site features dozens of links to other cool sites on the Web, all sorted by category. You can also get study help here if you need it by clicking on the Learning Center button. Once you get inside the Learning Center, you can learn about scholarship listings as well as get online tutoring or other homework help.

Another cool feature of Cyberkids is the chat rooms, where you can share opinions and ideas with kids from around the world.

Learn the secret behind a person's name

What's in a Name?

http://tqjunior.thinkquest.org/4626/first.htm

A person's name isn't just another word. It tells everybody who they are. Plus, with a little searching, people can discover the secret meanings of their names. Edward, for example, means "rich guardian." Other names, such as those for days, months, and even pets, have hidden meanings, too. The kids and adults who built the What's in a Name? site can help anyone learn what all these names mean.

The search starts with a click on a link for a category of names, such as First Names. There's a big list of boys' and girls' first names, from Albert and Amanda to Zachania and Zoe. The site's creators included a little history of each name. Who would have guessed the name Tiffany comes from the country of Greece?

The Last Names section lists the 25 most common last names in America. Kids can look for their last names on the list. The section on Famous Name Changers tells about well-known people who decided they wanted new names.

The Days section tells how important the Vikings and Romans were to the words people use today. These people, who lived a long time ago, named every day on our calendar. Most of the

First Names

WOW! It seems like everyone wants to see THEIR name on this page but that would be almost impossible!

Can't find the name you're looking for here? Try this link

Albert	Old German	noble, bright	First popular in England after the marriage of Victoria to Prince Albert in 1840.
Amanda	Latin	beloved	It shares its roots with Amy
Andrew	Greek	manly	Andre in French and Anders in Danish.
Ashley	Old English	a woods of ash trees	Originally a last name, Ashley can refer to a boy or girl.
Barbara	Greek & Latin	foreign,strange	Has lost its popularity since the 1960's.
Beatrice	Latin	bringing happiness	Shakespeare's heroine in Much Ado About Nothing.
Bradley	Old English	broad meadow	A last name that has become a popular first name.
Brandon	English	fiery hill	Originally a last name - from "brand" Old English for a torch
Calvin	Latin	bald	Calvin became a given name in honor of the Protestant reformer John Calvin
Caroline	Latin	giving	It is not from Carl, it is the feminine form of Charles!
Chelsea	Old English	river landing	Also a place name - and President Bill Clinton's daughter.
Clio	Greek	praise	Clio was the Greek muse of history.
Cooper	British?	barrel maker	Originally a last name. The original Latin form meant a "cask."
Daphne	Greek	from the plant "laurel"	Daphne was the Greek nymph changed into a laurel tree to escape from her Apollo who loved her.
Diana	Latin	divine	Roman moon goddess. Will certainly be popular after the 1997 death of Princess Diana.
Douglas	Gaelic	dark blue	Originally the name of a river, later a last name.
Dylan	Welsh	sea god	In Welsh legend the ocean wept when he died.
Edward	Old English	rich guardian	A popular name with British Kings.
Emily	Latin	eager	The name of a noble Roman family
Eric, Erik	Danish	ruler of all	?
Erica	Latin	scientific name for the plant heather	A feminine form of Eric.
Felix	Latin	happy	Popularly connected with the cartoon cat by that name and because it resembles the scientific word for cats
Fiona	Gaelic	fair, white	Has a large popularity in Great Britain.
Flora	Latin	flower	Variants of it include Florence and Floris.

Learn where your name comes from and what it means!

calendar's names came from gods, goddesses, or heroes of ancient times. Kids can talk like a Viking if they call Thursday "Thor's Day" instead.

LINKS:
Pet Names, Names for the Millennium, Requests From Guests, Beanie Baby Names

Online show-and-tell for kids

Kids Did This! Hotlist

http://sln.fi.edu/tfi/hotlists/kids.html

Looking at projects made by other kids is important for a couple of reasons. When kids compare work, they can see how their own projects stack up against the competition, and they can get new ideas for their next school assignments and

You can see what other kids are doing for *their* projects!

hobbies. The Kids Did This! Web site helps in both cases by gathering together a big group of projects from kids around the world. It's like a science fair, art show, and speech contest rolled into one.

Visitors start by selecting a category such as science, social studies, art, mathematics, or school newspapers. Clicking a category shows a list of all the kid-made projects inside. Some of the categories have 50 or more projects to look at. There are some great entries here, such as the stamps kids drew to honor Native Americans. Some of the kids' projects are activities like a site where kids can check out parts of a skeleton and be quizzed. This site is updated often, so there are always plenty of cool things to check out.

Remember that this site is mostly about fun stuff and isn't meant to be an authoritative source of information. These projects aren't from experts. Before anyone uses these reports for school projects, they should first check out and confirm the facts.

LINK:
Educational Hotlists

Chapter 2

Homework Help

Homework assignments would be a breeze if kids had an expert on every subject living in their home. These experts could provide tips on tough math problems, talk all about the planets in our solar system, or help with any other subject. However, most people probably don't have anyone *that* smart hanging around. In fact, there probably isn't one person anywhere who's an expert on *everything*.

Knowing how to use the Web provides access to all kinds of experts. The sites in this section are great for helping kids finish hard assignments whenever they get stuck. Kids can think of the Web as a huge, easy-to-use reference book.

But, unlike a book, the Web can talk back to kids. (Well, sort of.) Kids can send questions to experts all over the world through e-mail. Then the experts will write back to kids with answers to tough questions, making kids feel like real homework research pros. Some of the sites in this section even let kids have some fun while they learn. Kids might just turn studying into something they actually like doing!

The place to learn about famous folks

Biography.com

http://www.biography.com/find/find.html

Biography.com knows when Teddy Roosevelt was born. It knows where Florence Nightingale grew up. It even knows where President Clinton went to college. In fact, Biography.com can tell kids all about the life of almost any famous person. No matter who kids need to learn about, chances are they'll find them here. This site is a great resource when writing papers or doing other homework about famous people for school.

Just type a person's name in the Search box on the main page and hit Go! Then read all about that person's life story. Biography.com tells why these people are famous and lists important dates in their lives and what connections they had to other famous people. These biographies aren't just about people you read about in history books. Try looking up some of your favorite people—like Dr. Seuss. You'll find out that the doctor's real name is Theodore Seuss Geisel. Remember that lots of living people are covered at Biography.com. Look up names like Michael Jordan to learn more about current celebrities.

LINKS:
HistoryChannel.com, Biography television schedule

Teachers help kids at home on this site

Homework Help

http://www.startribune.com/ stonline/html/special/homework/

No really tough homework question can stump kids when they use a personal homework helper. The real-life teachers at the Homework Help site know about every school subject. They'll read kids' questions and send answers back to them.

Some answers are long; some just tell you where to look for answers. It depends on the teacher answering the question. Don't count on this site for help the night before a report is due, though. You will probably have to wait about 24 hours or longer for the answer. Make this a study tool, but not your only tool.

Click Elementary School Topics. Then go to the bottom of the page and click the Search button. Type in the topic you need help on, like "Christopher Columbus" or "snakes." You might find answers teachers have already given other kids on the same topic. If the search doesn't help, click a subject name on the left side of the screen, then keep choosing subjects until you find the right one. Then, questions and answers will appear.

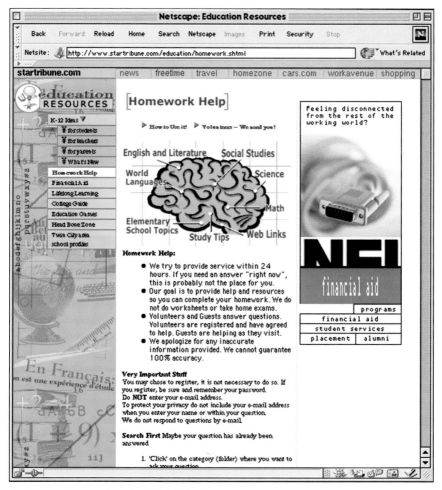

Need answers from real teachers? This is the place.

If kids want to ask their own questions, they can go to the bottom of the screen and click Add Discussion. Look for the teacher's answer the next day.

Dig into science

Exploratorium

http://www.exploratorium.edu/

Trying something sounds better than listening to someone talk about it. Take a look at Exploratorium. This site for

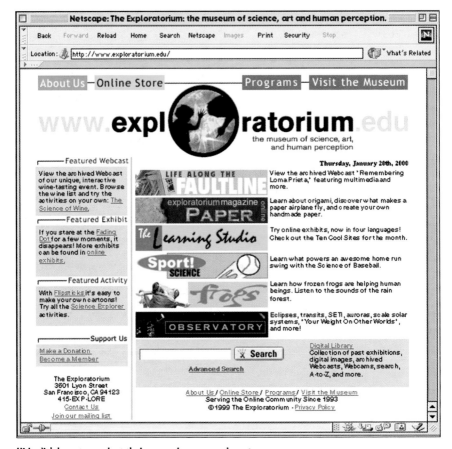

Kids click here to conduct their own science experiments.

curious kids is based on the Exploratorium museum in San Francisco, where visitors get to dig into science experiments. ExploraNet puts some of the best science exhibits and experiments online for kids to try. The site is updated monthly, but all of the old exhibits are archived; the deeper you dig on this site, the more cool things you are bound to find!

Visit some of the Exploratorium's great exhibits in The Digital Library. A few of the exhibits explain why people's eyes play tricks on them. Another exhibit discusses the effects of nuclear war. Another exhibit tells you all sorts of amazing facts about frogs and shows you pictures of frogs from all over the world!

The Learning Studio's Science Explorer section is packed with science activities for kids. Learn how to mix a solution that turns dingy old pennies into bright, shiny ones. Read the instructions for growing crystals in a bowl on a sunny shelf.

Special features explore areas like the shape of rocks in Death Valley National Park and how people's feet are the greatest sports equipment. For those kids who are not easily grossed out, follow along as a scientist dissects a real sheep's brain!

LINKS:
Institute For Inquiry, Exploratorium Events

Money makes this site go around

KidsBank.Com

http://www.kidsbank.com/index_2.html

Adults talk about money a lot, so it might seem like something that kids don't want to worry about. But money's important to everybody. Lots of kids earn money through allowances, lemonade stands, mowing lawns, or doing other jobs. Learning about money helps kids buy more with the money they have.

KidsBank.com helps young folks learn the basics of how money and banks work. Cartoon characters like Penny and Dollar Bill take users on tours of various money topics. Start with Penny, who explains important questions such as why we have money, who makes new coins and paper money, and whose pictures are on paper money. The information about bank topics such as earning interest is best for older kids. Whenever the Professor appears, click on him for in-depth lessons.

Kids can head to the game room to test how much they've learned and use calculators to figure out how long it takes to become a millionaire. They can send money questions to Mr. Money. He'll post an answer in a couple of days, and kids can read answers to other people's questions about topics such as credit cards and savings accounts.

Play games to learn geography

Geo-Globe: Interactive Geography

http://library.advanced.org/10157/

There's a lot more to geography than finding states on a map. Winners at this site's games will know about maps around the world as well as something about the earth's water, land, and animals.

Click Enter Geo-Globe on the main page to reach a list of the site's six games. They each use maps and pictures to test kids' knowledge of different geographical areas. In Geo-Find, kids name the locations of cities, countries, rivers, and mountains. Start with the beginner level, because the other levels get pretty hard!

Geo-Quest lets kids guess the name of a mystery animal. Get clues by asking questions about where the animal lives and how big it is. Geo-Seas covers the oceans. Geo-Tour lets kids follow clues to find famous landmarks. There are several other sections as well.

Funny sounds let kids know whether their answers are wrong or right, and links help them look up the answers they don't know right away. Even when kids get some answers wrong, Geo-Globe makes it easy to learn.

Explore our outer space neighbors

The Nine Planets–Just For Kids!

http://www.tcsn.net/afiner/

Don't blast off into an outer space homework assignment without voyaging to The Nine Planets. This site tells kids all about planets in our solar system, along with other things that zip around in space, such as asteroids, moons, and comets. The site's writing is geared toward older elementary grades, but anyone can enjoy the out-of-this-world photos and helpful links to other information.

Click each planet's name to get the basics about it, such as its size and surface temperature. (This is a metric site, so it lists measurements in kilometers and kilograms.) Kids will also read the stories of humans discovering and learning about each planet. The planet Pluto, for example, isn't named after a cartoon dog. It's named after a Roman god who supposedly lived in the underworld. This planet is so far from the sun's light that it reminded people of that mythological god.

A glossary explains spacey words such as "astronomical unit" so kids won't be confused. Some sections explain how planets and other space objects (moons, satellites, etc.) get their names and what mystery planets may still be undiscovered in space. Use links to learn about spacecrafts that have visited the planets.

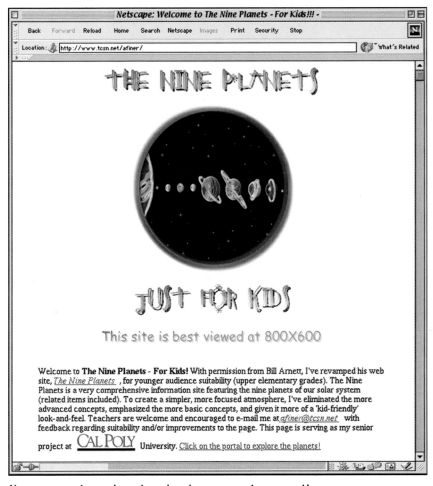

Almost any question you have about the solar system can be answered here.

LINKS:
Master Picture List, MarsWatch, NASA Spacelink, The Planetary Society

Do the math and take a swing at this site

Funbrain.com Math Baseball

http://www.funbrain.com/math/index.html

Practicing math is important, but it sure can be tough some-times. The next time kids need to practice addition, subtrac-tion, or other math, they can try playing baseball instead. Funbrain.com Math Baseball lets kids play a game at the same time they're practicing math.

When kids show up at this ballpark, they can pick the math skills they need to work on. Practice one task, such as multipli-cation, or several math skills at once. Then choose a skill level: easy, medium, hard, or super brain. The pitcher throws a math problem like "6×5=" at kids and if they answer it right, they'll get a single, double, triple, or home run (depending on how hard the question was). Children will see their baserunner heading around the bases. Kids are out if they miss a question. Kids might have such a good time playing baseball that they'll wind up practicing their math skills more than ever.

Funbrain helps kids practice other skills, too. Check out the Click Here For More Games link. Play Spell Check and spot the misspelled words. If a kid sees enough misspellings, he or she can put his or her name on the leader board.

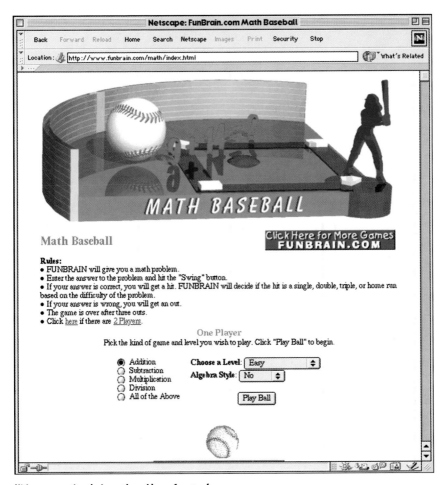

Kids can practice their math and have fun, too!

LINK:
More Games

Brush up on art knowledge and solve the big case

A. Pintura, Art Detective

http://www.eduweb.com/pintura

Famous art might seem kind of boring. After all, they're just pictures, right? But when kids know what to look for, every painting has a secret to tell. Kids will have to listen to those secrets to solve cases when they play A. Pintura, Art Detective. After finishing this adventure, designed for kids in fourth grade and up, kids will never look at "pictures" the same way again.

Fiona Featherduster has come for help in identifying a mysterious painting found in her grandfather's attic. She knows one of the six famous artists on her list painted it, but kids need to figure out which one. Artist names such as Raphael and Picasso may not mean much now, but kids will learn what each painter was known for as the case goes on. Picasso made over 20,000 paintings, but do the Picasso paintings on the Web page look like the mystery painting? Make a guess and see if Fiona thinks it is right.

By the end, kids will be able to match paintings with the artist who created them. They will even identify the mystery painting! Children will learn to like looking at art once they understand elements like composition and color in each painting.

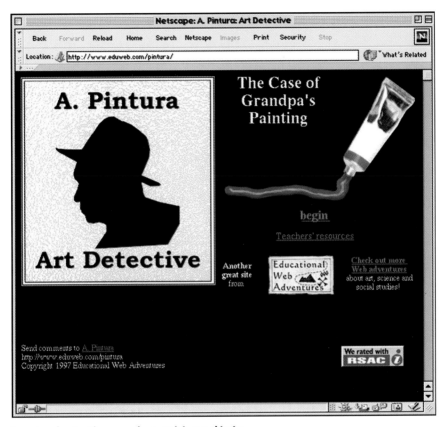

Learning about art is easy and entertaining on this site.

LINKS:
Teacher's Resources, Educational Web Adventures

A friend who has plenty of answers

Ask Jeeves for Kids

http://www.ajkids.com

When kids visit a big city, they need a friend to show them around. The Internet has more people on it than *any* big city, so people need a friend to give them directions there, too. Fortunately, you can ask Jeeves for help. Jeeves can answer almost any question about what's on the Web. This friendly butler lets kids ask questions in any words they want. He'll look around the Internet and show them where to find the answer.

Ask Jeeves for Kids is a search engine—a tool that can tell kids where to find information on the Web. Ask Jeeves is easy for kids to use because they can type in their question just as it comes into their head. Ask Jeeves, "How old is the moon?" and he'll show you questions he can answer on that topic, such as "Where can I get general information on the celestial body, the moon?" Click one of the questions to visit a site that has the answer. Jeeves does all the work and delivers the answer, acting just like a kid's own personal librarian.

Check Jeeves' Word of the Day to increase your vocabulary. Check out Cool Sites to find tons of cool links that you will want to check out. There is also a section for students as well as one for teachers that lists some interesting questions with answers.

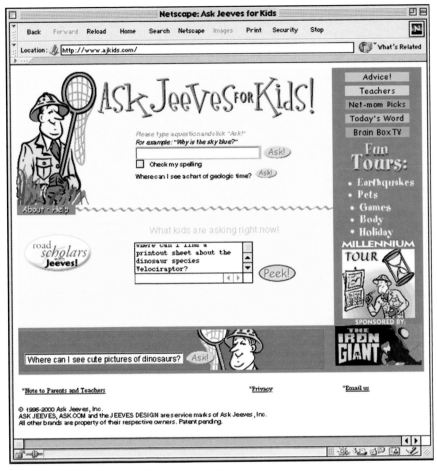

Jeeves can tell kids where to find information on the net.

LINKS:
Advice, Teachers, Net-Mom Picks, Today's Word, Brain Box

All kinds of experts help with kids' questions

Ask an Expert Sources

http://www.cln.org/int_expert.html

Nobody can be an expert at everything. Children just have to find the real experts and ask them questions. Try sending questions through the Web to a professional in any field. It's like finding a room full of smart people waiting to help.

The Ask an Expert Sources page puts kids in touch with all kinds of smart people. Kids can find help on subjects such as Math, Dinosaurs, Health, and Native American Culture. They'll talk to people like Dr. Math and Dr. Bug. The experts come from all over, so their rules for answering questions may differ. Some will write back to kids personally. Some will put the answer on a Web page. A lot of the experts list answers to the questions they get most, so an answer to your question may already be posted.

Make the expert's job easy when sending in a question. Kids can tell the experts their age and where they've already looked for information. Ask a specific question like, "Where do whales spend the winter?" instead of "Tell me about whales." This helps the experts answer questions clearly.

Remember: These experts aren't here to do kids' homework. Kids should only ask for help after looking for information themselves first.

See what happened on this date

This Day in History

http://www.historychannel.com/today/

It's hard to imagine what life was like way back in history. It might be easier to think about one day in history—maybe today's date in 1776, or 1950, for example. This Day in History shows children what important things happened on this very day throughout history.

When kids visit the site, one major event that happened on the current date is right at the top. There's usually a movie or audio clip to go with that event. Click a button to see what happened on this day in other years as well as a list of famous people born on this day. There are even lists of songs that were big hits on this day. Kids can check to see how many they have heard of before.

Users can look up their birthday and see the events listed there. They can also find out which famous people share their birthday. When working on a school history project, kids can look up the day they're writing about and add that extra information to their report. Kids might know that the Declaration of Independence was approved on July 4, 1776, but what *else* happened on that day throughout history?

LINKS:
The History Channel, Great Speeches, Classroom, History Store

Get to know U.S. presidents

A Presidential Exploration

http://library.advanced.org/11492/index2.html

One job in America is so tough to get that only 41 people have ever done it (several have served more than one term), even though our country is more than 220 years old. Being President of the United States is a special job, and kids can find out what it's like at A Presidential Exploration.

Use the Oval Office link to look up information on a certain president. Each section tells kids what happened to a president while he was in office and lists what he did while he had the job.

The Convention link describes what it takes to be president. First, potential presidents must be at least 35 years old. Then they have to get people to vote for them in an election. Kids will also learn that the president has a lot of power, but he can't just do *anything* he wants. Learn the rules every president has to follow.

This site shows you not only the history of the presidency, but also how a president gets elected. Did you know that candidates for president spend most of their time traveling around the country—some of them for two or three years before the election?

Everything about the presidency–the people and the job–is explained here.

When kids get tired of studying, they can have fun with their presidential knowledge in the Rec. Room. Four games here test how much kids know about presidential facts and pictures. The Presidents Quiz is the easiest one. Tackle multiple-choice questions such as, "Which president is known as the Father of his Country?"

Quick facts are just a few clicks away

Encyclopedia.com

http://www.encyclopedia.com

It would take a room full of books to hold all the information that kids can pull up on the computer screen when visiting Encyclopedia.com. This site lets kids read the articles in a whole set of encyclopedias without ever opening a book. The 14,000 articles here tell children about almost any topic they can come up with. When just getting started on a topic, look here for the basics (for example, to find out when George Washington Carver was born).

To start a search, just point to the book that has the letter of the subject in question. For example, when looking for information about President Abraham Lincoln, click the L book, then look through the list to find Abraham Lincoln's name. Click it to read a short article about this great man. Use the links to visit other sites packed with more information on related topics.

Kids follow similar steps to look up articles about everything from apes to zoology. Or, to avoid just browsing around, go right to the topic by using the Search window on the main page. Type in the desired topic and click Find It! for a list of articles to read.

LINKS:
Infonautics, Related Internet Sites

Where to find help for any homework assignment

Study Web

http://www.studyweb.com/

Here's a place to find help on almost any topic. The Study Web site rounds up all kinds of sites and sticks them in categories. That makes it easy for kids to quickly find the help they need.

Let's say a teacher asked students to find out where computers came from. Go to Study Web and click Computer Science. Then click History Of Computers. A big list of sites with information on that topic will then pop up on the screen. Choose A Brief History Of Computers or another site. In an unrelated search, kids could also pick something like Animals & Pets, then choose Endangered Species, then Alligators. A search tool lets kids type in the words they're looking for and jump right to the information.

Study Web tells kids a little about each site, so it's easy to pick the best one. It ranks each Web site for a grade level, such as "5+." That means that particular site is for any kid in fifth grade or higher.

Be sure to try the Study Buddy link. This helpful resource provides a little reference window with a dictionary.

LINKS:
Resource Directory, The Classroom Internet

If it's gross and gooey inside you, it's explained here

Your Gross & Cool Body

http://www.yucky.com/body

Some weird things happen inside people's bodies. Bumpy, gurgling sounds rumble deep in our stomachs. Sometimes bad breath scares everybody away. Then there's the gross stuff kids

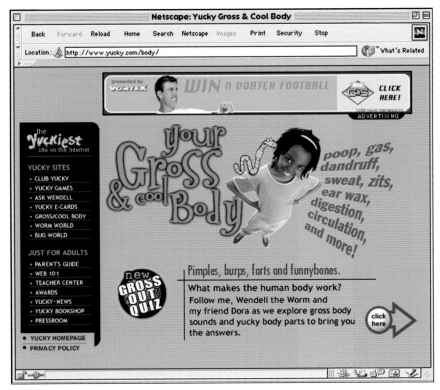

If it's too gross to ask a friend, this site will answer kids' questions.

don't even talk about. These are normal body actions, and kids have a right to know why they happen. "The Yuckiest Site on the Internet" tells kids why all this stuff is going on.

Click on the arrow next to Dora to go to the next screen, which will feature a list of topics to Dora's right. Kids can learn about whatever body part they want by aiming the pointer at the name of that feature. Click Stinky Pits to learn why armpits can smell bad. Kids will learn where all kinds of gross stuff comes from, including dandruff, belches, and hiccups.

> The body can be yucky and gross sometimes, but it's all great science! Everything that your body produces has a purpose. This site is a great way to learn all about how your body works—and have icky fun while you're at it!

Sections on each body part let kids get the answers to questions like "Why do we vomit?" and "Why is vomit green?" Fun Facts tell kids more about things—like, for instance, how flies use vomit to eat. Wendell the Worm, an ace reporter, answers any questions kids send in. There are also lots of cool and icky sound effects on this site.

"The Yuckiest Site on the Internet" can explain about all kinds of stuff. There are special sections on bugs and even worms. Kids can read about parasites called tapeworms that live inside of animals—and sometimes even people!

A library full of knowledge to help with homework

KidsClick!

http://sunsite.berkeley.edu/KidsClick!

When you have a homework question, who is the best person to ask? A librarian, of course! This site was put together by librarians to make it easy for kids to use the Web to find answers. And like any good teacher, this site doesn't just give you the answer—it points you in the right direction and lets *you* do the work.

There are lots of ways to find answers at this site. You can put a word or two in the search field and the site will come back with lots of links to sites that hold the answer. Or you can look at the categories of sites that the librarians have listed to find links to the subject you're interested in. If you're doing a paper on the Civil War, for example, you could click on American History and then try Civil War, Abraham Lincoln, or slavery.

Next to each link there is a short description of the site. The listings also tell you what reading level the site is geared to, so you can look at only the best sites for your age group.

> Librarians are always a great source of information for kids doing homework. At KidsClick!, kids have access to hundreds of librarians, eager to guide them to the best resources on the Web. All of the sites listed at KidsClick! have been reviewed by librarians to make sure they're safe for kids.

The features here add up to math-mania

The Math Forum Student Center

http://forum.swarthmore.edu/students/

No question is too hard or too simple for Dr. Math. This wizard of numbers will answer almost any math question kids send in through e-mail. He can answer beginner questions like "Does 1+1 make 2 or 11?" He also tackles harder topics, such as explaining commutative and inverse properties.

No matter what the topic, his answers are always clear enough to help kids do better in math class. All the homework help at The Math Forum Student Center can help students do better on the next big math exam. Click Elementary on the main page to get information especially for kids ages 5 to 11. When kids have a specific problem to solve, they can go straight to Ask Dr. Math. If they're just looking for ways to brush up on skills, they can try different exercises around the site.

The Math Tips & Tricks are especially handy. These secrets teach kids to do math faster than a calculator. Tips here explain fast ways to multiply by 9 or 5 and how to decide what numbers are divisible by 3. With practice, and these expert ideas, kids can turn into real math masters.

Answers to the homework questions that kids ask the most

KidsConnect:
Frequently Asked Questions

http://www.ala.org/ICONN/kcfaq.html

FAQs, which stands for Frequently Asked Questions, are online sites that answer questions for users. There's a good chance that if kids are wondering about something, it's explained in a FAQ. The KidsConnect FAQs answer homework questions kids have most often. The answers come from professional librarians.

KidsConnect groups FAQs by subject. In the subjects, choose from areas such as history, science, news, and animals. Click a subject to see questions such as "Why do leaves change colors in the fall?" Click the question to read the answer. In the topics area, you can get help on specific topics like earthquakes or Martin Luther King, Jr.

The librarians don't give full answers, but their tips tell kids where to find the answers. The librarians always explain how they found the information on the Net and in the library. Kids should read that part of the answer so they can learn how to search the Web on their own.

If the FAQs don't answer every question, click the e-mail address at the bottom of the page for more help. Kids can

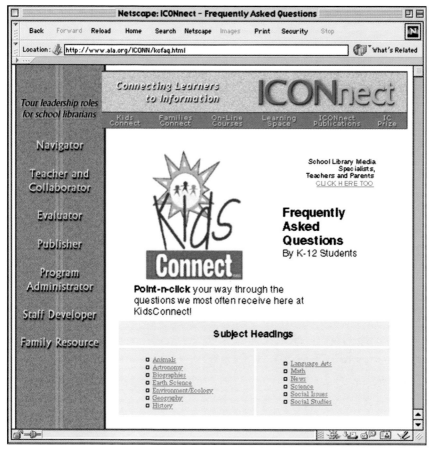

Does your question get asked a lot? KidsConnect will lead you to the answer.

send their questions to a librarian and get an answer back within two school days.

LINKS:
ICONnect, American Library Association

Chapter 3

Online Activities

Kids can think of the Web as a giant library. It lets them look up information on almost any topic. But the Web is more exciting than a regular library. It brings thousands of hands-on activities right to a user's computer screen. Kids can access video game arcades, coloring books, storybooks, card shops, and much more on their computers.

Kids will find some games that they've played before. They might try to shoot a basketball through a hoop or sink the computer's aircraft carrier in a game of Battleship. But other Web games take children on new adventures. Cybersurfari and Headbone Derby make them detectives, searching for clues all over the Internet. And that turf just keeps expanding.

The most interesting online activities let kids try things they couldn't anywhere else. Ever send a musical birthday card to a friend? At the Blue Mountain Arts card shop, kids can send virtual cards that play cartoons and music through e-mail to friends and family. And best of all, these fun cards are free.

Kids don't just watch this channel

The Kid's Channel

http://members.tripod.com/~kid_channel/index.htm

Kids will feel welcome right away at The Kid's Channel. When they type in their names, they'll see a personalized message. Then they can go on in and read a story, send postcards to friends, try recipes, or play games. Best of all, kids help build the site by sending in their own creations.

Kid authors are ready to entertain users with stories and jokes at this site. Click the Stories button to read tales kids sent in such as "The Lost Dog" by 9-year-old Samantha. Jokes come straight from kids, too, and users can send in their own stories or jokes with the e-mail button. The Recipes section isn't just about food; it also tells kids how to make some neat crafts, such as their own stickers. The Art Work section shows off pictures kids send in, and users can send in their own pictures to enter a monthly contest.

Try out a real "antique" video game in the Games area. Pong is an electronic ping-pong game, and it's been around so long that some kids' parents might have played it when *they* were young! Challenge them to a game and see who gets the better score.

LINKS:
Kid's Cooking Corner, KID STUFF, Kids Korner

Younger kids have fun learning here

Enchanted Learning Software

http://www.enchantedlearning.com/

Kids just getting into reading can dig into an electronic toy box at the Enchanted Learning Software site. The activities here are just right for youngsters who are learning to read and beginning to discover everything around them.

The Little Explorers book link is a good place to start. This dictionary shows pictures of words starting with each letter of the alphabet. Click "K," for example, to see a kangaroo, kitten, keyboard, and more. Most of the words have links with more information on the object. This is a fun place to practice reading.

Neat stuff on the main page includes bird and dinosaur jokes, a connect-the-dots game, nursery rhymes, a truck game, and an entire section on panda bears!

Zoom Topics let kids check out places such as The Great Wall of China, Australia, Japan, and the United States. They can follow the links all over the pages to read whatever they think is most interesting. Zoom Topics on Countries teach users about the animals and history of the country, plus they show kids how to make crafts from each country. Japan's craft is especially cool: It shows kids how to make animals out of folded paper (origami).

LINKS:
Alive! Excellence in Education, Cool Safe Links for Kids, Parents and Teachers

There's something for every youngster here.

An online funhouse packed with fun stuff

Bonus.com

http://www.bonus.com

Bonus.com turns a kid's computer into an electronic playground. This colorful site, packed with games, sounds, and cool graphics, really is a "SuperSite for Kids," just like it says.

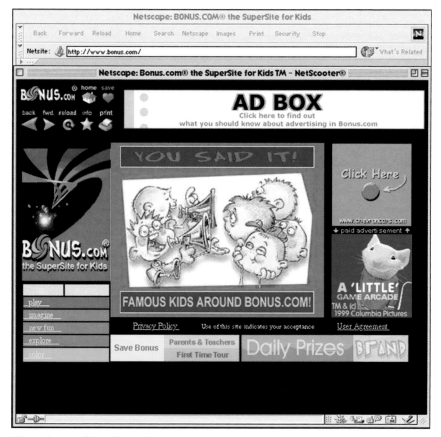

This site is a real "bonus" for kids!

The games are worth a visit all by themselves. Click the New Fun button on the main page and then click the Top 10 button to see the most popular games. Kids can test their skills at blasting aliens in Alien Wars or help girls hit the basket in Girls' Superdunk. Make some computer art at DrawBots and e-mail it to a friend.

Users never know what will show up on their screens in the Imagine area. You can look up great recipes, find out about the latest kid celebrities, or research almost anything—this section is always changing, just like peoples' imaginations!

The Explore section points kids to great lessons on all kinds of topics. They can read about things like why Leonardo da Vinci was so important, read current news headlines, check out the I Can Be Anything site, or view national flags from countries around the world.

You can go to the Color section and paint lots of stuff. Learn about great artists in the Cool Art section. You can also take fun quizzes from Cybert or look at animals doing some weird and wild things! There are also plenty of chances for kids to color pictures, get craft ideas, and read about animals. Bonus.com has so much to see that kids will keep coming back.

The computer will try to guess the animal in a kid's imagination

Animal Guessing Game

http://www.bushnet.qld.edu.au/animal

For once, kids are the ones giving the quiz, not the ones taking it. In the Animal Guessing Game, the kids already know all the answers, and the computer is the one trying to guess. The user's job is to think of an animal—any one they want. Then the computer asks the user questions as it tries to guess the animal that he sees in his imagination.

Don't tell the computer what the animal is when visiting the site! Kids should just type in their name so the computer knows who they are. Then the computer starts asking kids questions like "Can the animal fly?" or "Is it a very small animal?" Kids should make sure they know a lot about the animals they're thinking of. The computer asks some hard questions like "Does it like to chew bones?" When kids run out of animals to stump the computer, they can look around the Internet and learn about new animals. Then they can come back to this Web site and play again.

Sometimes the computer can't guess the animal in the kid's mind. Then the user should tell the computer a little about the animal so it can do a better job of guessing when the next kid thinks of that creature.

LINKS:
BushNet Home Page, BushScene, Earth Science Australia

For a change, let the computer do the talking

Read-along Stories

http://www.indiana.edu/~eric_rec/fl/pcto/read.html

Learning to read is a tough job, but the Read-along Stories site makes it a little easier. This online storybook has some cool tales to tell, plus a narrator's voice will read the story aloud with kids. That way they can follow along and hear someone else say any hard words they can't figure out.

And if kids aren't in the mood to read, they can just listen to the narrator's voice. It's almost like having a real person read the story!

The site has a lot of different stories. In one tale, Emily explores the world with magic jelly beans. They help her travel to events such as baseball games and even to places like Mexico. In another, Anne enters a forest to look for a scary monster called a Grindelstark. Another story tells about a boy who meets a bunch of angry cows. Fun pictures help kids follow along with each story.

Click the words at the top and bottom of the page for ideas of things to think about before and after reading each tale. At the end of the story about cows, for example, kids can think about why people should be kind to animals.

LINK:
Parents and Children Online

Kids will find lots of fun ways to pass the time with author Dav Pilkey

Dav's Page O' Fun

http://www.pilkey.com/dpfstart.htm

If your idea of fun is jokes, paper airplanes, and mazes (and whose isn't?), you'll have a blast at Dav's Page O' Fun. Writer and cartoonist Dav Pilkey is a grown-up with a kid's sense of fun. His Web site is full of the kind of games that kids like best. On the jokes page, you'll find some old faves and some great new ones to crack up your friends. (What kind of mosquitoes live at the North Pole? Cold ones.) For more online fun, take a drawing lesson, answer some trivia questions, or solve a crossword puzzle.

There's plenty of fun at Dav Pilkey's page.

Kids who like Pilkey's books, including *The Adventures of Captain Underpants* and *The Paperboy,* will enjoy getting to know a little more about the award-winning author and how he got started in his career. Kids have a choice when they read Pilkey's story about himself, "The Almost Completely True Adventures of Dav Pilkey"–they can read the old-fashioned version (words only) or the cartoon version.

If you prefer your fun away from the computer, you can print out the mazes, word games, and connect-the-dots games and play them later or share them with your friends. The games have three levels of difficulty (from "Easy Sneezy" to "Difficult Schmifficult") so kids can find the one that's right for them.

Dav also offers drawing lessons (which you can either do online or offline). If you want special holiday cards, you can go to the Print 'N' Color section and print out great Dav drawings.

Are paper airplanes your thing? Check out the directions to make the Perfectly Portable Pilkey-Powered Paper Pilot "Pug Plane" (say that three times fast). You'll certainly be the only kid on the block with this paper airplane extraordinaire! And if paper airplanes are too run-of-the-mill, check out the Krazy Kopters.

Send virtual presents from this site

Virtual Flowers and Gifts

http://www.en.com/users/felion/index.html

It's the thought that counts. Here's a way to send cool presents without spending any money. The Virtual Flowers and Gifts site lets kids pick a great virtual present and send it through an e-mail message. Kids are really just sending a picture of something like flowers or a car, but they can pretend that the gift is real.

This site is perfect for making a friend's day with a fun message. If a pal really wants a sports car, get them one from this site. Kids might send one of these presents to Mom and Dad at work to let them know they're thinking about them.

This gift shop has presents for everybody on a child's list. Choose a bunch of online flowers, type a special message like "Happy Birthday, Mom!", and send it in an e-mail message. Sometimes music can be added.

Flowers aren't for everybody, so look through the list for other gifts. Kids might want to send a virtual apple pie, virtual hugs and kisses, or an Awesome Award to somebody special.

A big arcade packed with online games

Bonnie's Fun Things to Do on the Computer

http://www2.arkansas.net/~mom/bonnie.html

When kids need an online expert to show them what's fun on the Web, they should go see Bonnie. She uses her site to point out the best (and most fun) kid activities around. There are enough cool ideas to keep kids busy surfing the Web for weeks. Bonnie helps kids find stories to read, recipes to try, and things to do when they're not using the PC. Some of her best pointers suggest games to play all over the Web. Kids click Play a Game and then choose Play an Easy Game or Play a Harder Game to get activities that match their skill levels. Everybody will be able to find a game that's right for them.

The Easy Games are perfect for younger kids. Try Hoot's Jigsaw Puzzle to put together a "cool" puzzle. Play Tic-Tac-Toe with Mario from the Nintendo games. He gives kids the "X," so they get to make the first move!

Bonnie shows kids where to give their brains a tougher workout in the section of harder games. Some are online versions of games kids might already play, such as Battleship. Kids can try to sink the computer's battleship before it sinks theirs. Or try a game of Hangman and guess the secret word before the stickman runs out of time.

LINKS:
Send a Card, Sing a Song, Holiday Fun

Cybersleuths scour the Web for clues in this detective game

CyberSurfari

http://www.cybersurfari.org

Good detectives needed! If kids think they can solve a mystery with clues spread around the world, then they may be ready to go on a CyberSurfari. This online treasure hunt sends kids on

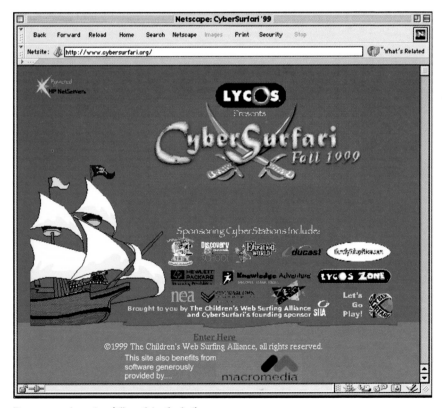

Try out your detective skills at CyberSurfari!

a mission to find information spread around the Web. Pay attention to the clues and have your Web skills ready.

The first official contest ran during fall 1998, and a new season began in March 2000. Play alone or get some classmates together to make a team. There are also practice questions on the home page to keep young cybersleuths busy in the event you miss the start of the contest.

Here's how it works. Kids will read clues listing the treasure that they are after and where to find it. Follow the links to the sites that have the information hiding somewhere inside. Dig up the right information and get a secret treasure code. Whoever finds the most treasure codes wins. Questions might point kids to a space exploration page, so they can find out how much a space shuttle carries. Clues might lead kids to find out what vegetable was carved as the first jack-o'-lantern.

While it's important for kids to use good Web skills, it's also important for them to use good teamwork skills, intelligence, and common sense. All these things will help you in the CyberSurfari.

One important thing to remember about this site is that the mysteries are seasonal. The contests keep changing along with the weather!

LINKS:
Excited Players!, How to Play

An online arcade that makes learning fun

JumpStart Kids Game Center

http://www.kidspace.com/kids/games/

If you get bored with the video games you own, go online. This site collects a bunch of games in an arcade where kids can play for free. Be ready to think while you play. These games will help you practice your math and reading skills while you're having fun. (Don't worry; this is more fun than any homework.)

Choose a game from the main page and wait for it to load. After you've downloaded the game and logged in, read the instructions on the left side of the screen. The games are simple enough that every kid should find a couple to play. Gamers don't need quick hands to play the basic games. A tile game has kids slide parts of a picture around until the picture comes together. Another good game for younger kids puts them to work solving simple math problems to connect dots.

Get ready for quick thinking in games like the Frog Well, where kids shoot a frog's tongue at the numbers needed to complete math problems. The Lemonade Stand game shows kids how hard it can be to run a business. Kids decide how much lemonade to make each day and what to charge for each cup. Watch the weather forecast! Cloudy days slow down sales.

LINKS:
Knowledge Adventure, 3-D Dinosaur Adventure

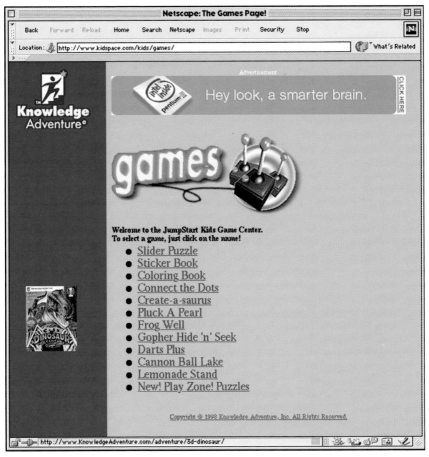

Find a new batch of video games here!

Join the race to find facts online

Headbone Derby

http://www.headbone.com/derby/

The race is on, and the slowest kid in school or the smallest person in class could beat everyone else in the Headbone Derby. The winner is whoever's best at digging up facts on the Internet. In the Internet Research Adventures, kids help comic strip characters Iz and Auggie gather information to solve their cases. Read the comics to follow the story, then jump in when the heroes need some information.

Assignments take Iz and Auggie around the earth and into outer space. Players might be looking for secrets of solar power in one episode and the names of musical composers or Martian canyons in another. Kids need to figure out where to look for the important information.

Sign up for a free Headbone Zone membership (alone or as part of a team) to join the derbies. As kids gather each piece of information from the Internet (or anywhere else), they'll earn points that can help them win great prizes like software and toys. When kids get stumped, they can always ask for a hint. But getting hints takes points off a team's score, as does sending in a wrong answer. Kids should make sure they have the right facts before sending in their guesses.

LINKS:
Prizes, Headbone Zone, Ecology Strikes Back!

Adopt a pretend pet and take care of it

Virtual Puppy

http://www.virtualpuppy.com

You can keep a pet inside a computer! This isn't some new kind of crazy insect that survives on electronic signals. These are computer programs that kids care for, just like real pets. The virtual puppies and kitties are like the digital toys that kids all over have been taking care of. The puppies and kitties don't have all of the animation of real pets, but caring for them is sort of realistic and fun.

Kids can adopt and name a puppy or kitty for free. Then they must visit their pet online to make sure they are happy, well fed, healthy, and clean. If the number score for any area gets too low, the caretaker must do something. Kids can click a few buttons to feed their pets, clean up after them, or even play with them. If pet owners forget to take care of their animals, it could be bad news for the new pets!

If you are thinking about getting a real pet, try adopting a virtual puppy or kitty first. These electronic animals aren't quite like the real thing, but if you can take care of one of these pets, you might be ready for a real one.

LINKS:
Virtual Kitty, Mail-a-Pup

The ultimate electronic clubhouse for kids

KidsCom

http://www.kidscom.com/

Lots of kids build clubhouses or tree houses where they can hang out with their friends and play games. KidsCom is like one of those clubhouses—on the Internet! It's a perfect place for kids from all over to hang out, make friends, and have a great time. Anyone can join for free.

Click Make New Friends to meet other cool kids. Kids can sign up for key pals (pen pals who kids talk to through e-mail) interested in the same things they are. Go into the Graffiti Wall chat area to have live, typed "conversations" on the screen. The adults working for KidsCom make sure that no bad guys get into the Graffiti Wall.

KidsCom helps make sure that adults—really important ones—listen to what the kids have to say. The Voice to the World section lets kids send messages about things like the environment and world hunger straight to the people running whole countries—including the United States. Users can tell other kids what they think by clicking the Kids Talk About section and posting messages about poll topics or even about their pets.

Then, kids can cut loose with some online video games or stretch their imaginations by writing stories they can send in with the click of a button.

Here's a cool place to hang out with kids from all over.

Send fun electronic cards

Blue Mountain Arts

http://www.bluemountain.com/

It's fun getting birthday cards, but don't they all pretty much look the same? What if kids could get a card that plays music

Come see some great cards.

and shows their names in big dancing letters? It's all possible at the Blue Mountain Arts site, which lets anybody send great electronic cards (for a birthday, graduation, vacation, or any other special event) for free.

Lots of Web sites let you send digital postcards with a picture and a message you type. But this site's cards are more fun because they add cartoons and sounds. Send friends an e-mail message saying that they have cards at the Blue Mountain site. When they open a card, they can see a greeting such as the one with jumping frogs playing a birthday song. Kids can show their parents how great they think they are by sending them a musical Best-Ever-Dad or Amazing Mom certificate.

There's even a calendar with a listing of holidays or celebrations. Did you know that National Hugging Day is January 21? This card shop has greetings for almost any occasion, including saying thank you, welcoming someone back from a trip, or even for regular holidays. Special sections offer cards with themes like wolves or horses or Boy Scouts or Girl Scouts. These musical cards are a great way to show someone you're thinking of them; plus, it's fun for kids to pick their own greetings.

LINKS:
Blue Mountain Poetry Contest, Card Pickup Window

Play with wild animals on this site

Sedgwick County Zoo Fun Stuff

http://www.scz.org/fun/right.html

All kids are welcome to tour the Sedgwick County Zoo in Wichita, Kansas—even if they're not there in person! All the games, tours, puzzles, quizzes, and other activities at this Web page relate to the animals living at the zoo.

The games send kids on safaris to find animals hiding in puzzles. The Jungle Adventure page takes you through the museum's Jungle exhibit. You can learn the names of the animals at the zoo on the Animal Names page.

If you just want to play, go to the games section and start printing out pages! On the site, there are several different types of puzzles to try, including one in which you have to connect the dots to draw a zoo animal. You can also test your animal IQ with quizzes. Who Am I? is an animal guessing game. Kids get a clue about an animal (such as, "I am considered King of the Beasts") and then are asked to guess the animal's name. Check the answers in the boxes below each question.

Finally, try the multimedia page, where you can check out the Swingin' with the Apes slide show and the zoo jukebox.

Stories on the computer really come alive here

Children's Storybooks Online

http://www.magickeys.com/books/index.html

When it's time for a story, kids don't always have to grab a book off the shelf. Visit Children's Storybooks Online. This little electronic library is full of all kinds of great tales about animals, adventures, and even the alphabet. There are stories for kids of all ages. Little readers can learn about things such as the sounds farm animals make, and older kids can check out adventures such as the story of Sliver Pete, the Old West cowpoke. Kids will find stories here about ponds, fairy tales, animals, and even strange creatures called wumpalumps.

Every story has great pictures. Some even move around, so kids should make sure they keep their eyes open for jumping gorillas and planes flying loop-de-loops. A few sound effects even pop up here and there.

Be sure to read the story about Buzzy Bee, the site's most popular character. The middle of the main page features a couple of Buzzy Bee riddles and a maze game. Pictures from the Buzzy story are in the Buzzy Bee Coloring Book, so kids can print the pictures and color them.

LINKS:
The Continuing Story, The Littlest Knight, It Could Happen

Games that let kids use their imaginations

MaMaMedia

http://www.mamamedia.com

This site is so packed with games and activities, it's impossible to list them all. The goal of MaMaMedia is for kids to learn to use the Web creatively—and as you'll see, creativity can be a whole lot of fun. At MaMaMedia, you don't just play games, you make them! Solving the Mindbender word puzzle is a blast, but making your *own* puzzle is even more fun.

You can do all sorts of things at the MaMaMedia site.

The paintings, puzzles, and word games are just the beginning. Budding authors with a story to tell should go to What's the Story and write a script to go along with the animated characters they set on stage. And if you think plain old drawings are too boring, check out Stamps and Stomps, where you can make pictures come alive with animation and sound.

Kids can make MaMaMedia very personal by designing the site to suit their tastes or moods. You can choose your own background, pick from some jazzy buttons, and create your own "Dig Sig," a digital caricature of yourself. And if you're in a different mood tomorrow, change it again!

If you like sending e-mail to your friends, why not take it one step further and create an animated greeting card? At Card Zapper, you can make a card to celebrate a holiday or birthday—or even "Happy Backwards Day!" Once you've made your card, send it off to a friend for a surprise.

There are also jokes, contests, an online magazine, and even a club to sign up for. Clicking on the Play button also allows you to design your own personal MaMaMedia screen—so you go right to your favorite places when you sign on!

LINKS:
Grownups, MaMaMedia Magazine, Contest

Chapter 4

Explore the World

The jungle rains are dripping on big, green leaves. There's a lion roaring just over the next hill. The smoke's so thick from the volcano belching fire over the treetops that the giant iceberg sliding closer almost sneaks by!

Icebergs in a jungle? The only way to visit a place *this* wild is through a computer. The Web sites in this chapter provide kids a ticket to every part of the earth after just a few minutes of Web surfing.

Sultry rain forests and frozen icebergs sit on pages right next to each other. Audio and video clips make it seem like kids really have stepped into exotic locations.

Of course, there is a lot more to see in the world than just nature. The Web provides tours of famous museums such as The Smithsonian Institution and landmarks like the White House. Other expeditions include visits to people living in other countries across the oceans. Spending some time in other countries teaches kids that people may do things differently, but also that all of us have a lot in common!

Visit wild animals without leaving your room

St. Louis Zoo

http://www.stlzoo.org/home.asp

The animals are all ready for a visit, so there's no reason to wait. Kids can drop by the St. Louis Zoo site to try out lots of neat activities and gather information. The St. Louis Zoo's Web site is a good one to explore, but it can also show what's available at zoo sites in general.

A lot of the information at this site comes in handy when planning a real visit to the St. Louis Zoo. But all the online animal information provides a zoo visit even for kids who never go to St. Louis. Visitors click the Animals button to see a zoo map, then click an area to visit. There are photos of each animal and information to read about how they live.

Links on the main page provide visitors with special zoo news. In the springtime, there are stories about new baby animals. The Kids link is the shortcut to information made just for young people. Fun activities include animal picture puzzles and coloring pages. There's also a chance to read up on animals that might be living in your backyard, as well as what you can do to help them. Stories go behind the scenes to teach about topics like how zookeepers spend their days.

LINKS:
Learning, Conservation/Research, Group Fun

Dig into the history of ancient Egypt

Pyramids, The Inside Story

http://www.pbs.org/wgbh/nova/pyramid

Not many of us will ever be lucky enough to visit the Great Pyramids of Egypt, one of the seven wonders of the world. But with the help of technology, we can now take a virtual trip deep down the corridors and passageways of three pyramids and the Sphinx.

The site's special photography allows kids to travel down into the pyramids and look around, up, and down the passageways with a 360-degree view. And they can get a bird's eye view of the plateau of Giza, where all the pyramids are, in a video flyover. For each pyramid, kids can also see a cross-section picture that shows them where all the passages lead. They can also read a history of that pyramid.

There's a lot to learn here, and not just about the pyramids. By following news flashes from an actual archeological dig,

We all know the Pyramids are big, but it's hard to imagine just how big they are by looking at a photo. How would they look stacked up against some of our tallest modern structures? Check out the drawing that compares Khufu to some modern structures, including the Statue of Liberty and Big Ben.

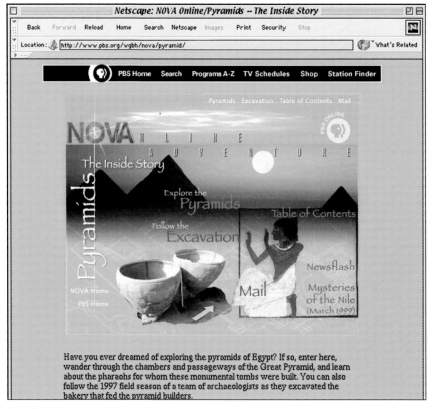

Have you ever dreamed of exploring the pyramids of Egypt? If so, enter here, wander through the chambers and passageways of the Great Pyramid, and learn about the pharaohs for whom these monumental tombs were built. You can also follow the 1997 field season of a team of archaeologists as they excavated the bakery that fed the pyramid builders.

Travel back thousands of miles–and years!

kids will find out about the people who built the pyramids (some think it took about 20,000 people to build them!), and the pharaohs they built them to honor. Ancient Egyptians had their own written language, called hieroglyphics, which kids can try to decode. With a few hints about what the symbols stand for, kids can go on their own archeological dig and uncover secret messages. There's even free software for kids to download and view.

LINKS:
Pyramids, Excavation

Go behind the scenes with a panda bear family

San Diego Zoo Panda Cam

http://www.sandiegozoo.org/special/pandas/ pandacam/index.html

It's not every day that a giant panda has a baby. In fact, there's been only one born in the entire Western hemisphere since 1990, and that happened in August, 1999, at the San Diego Zoo. Even if you don't live near San Diego, you can go visit the baby and her parents at this site, which has live camera shots of the bears' den. The video images are updated every few minutes, so you can get an up-close picture of the pandas as they go about their business.

To learn more about the baby, kids can check out the regular news flashes detailing the stages of the baby's life from the moment she was born. By reading the daily updates, kids learn the habits of pandas and how they take care of their young. Kids can also watch the baby grow up through a series of adorable photos and videos, ranging from the time she was a tiny, hairless wonder to the present, when she begins to look

Once you've visited the zoo, why not send a postcard to a friend? From the site you can send a digital postcard with a picture of the adorable panda baby. And if you'd rather send a picture of another animal, go wild! There are lots of animals to choose from, including bears, birds, reptiles, and marsupials.

like her mother, Bai Yun. Kids can learn lots of fun panda facts here, too. Did you know that pandas have bad eyesight? Or that giant pandas weigh up to 350 pounds? Because there are only about 1,000 pandas left in the world, it is important that we learn as much about them as possible.

LINKS:
Panda Facts, Multimedia

See what the pandas are up to at this site!

Frankly, one of the best museums on the Web

The Franklin Institute Science Museum

http://sln.fi.edu/

Visiting the Franklin Institute Science Museum's Web site is almost as good as visiting a museum in person. The awesome exhibits here cover every area of science, from earthquakes to living things to old Ben Franklin himself. The best part? This museum is open whenever kids want to visit!

The Earthforce link offers "moving" lessons on how the earth constantly shakes, rattles, and rolls because of forces like earthquakes, volcanoes, and tidal waves. Articles explain what would happen if people could dig a hole all the way to the center of the earth. They'd find burning rock! This exhibit tells how that hot rock moves around to create volcanoes. Links on every topic help users explore the information as much as they want.

The online exhibit about a human heart is especially interesting. It pays to know all about this special pump that keeps people alive. A special report explains the heart's job. "Bio-point" is a free pass to drop in on a real science class as it tackles projects like dissecting a crayfish. The pictures help kids follow along just as if they're in the lab.

Fascinating facts and fun can be found at the Franklin Institute's site.

LINKS:

Educational Hotlists, Math Problems (updated monthly), 175 Years of Science!

Tour foreign lands with the kids who live there

Let's Go!: Around the World

http://www.ccph.com/

Everybody's neighborhood is a little different, but for kids living in places like the Amazon rainforest or Africa, life is very different. Visitors can hang out with some of these kids for a while at the Let's Go!: Around the World site to see how their lives are different from those of American kids.

Clicking the frog starts a visit to the rain forest; clicking the cheetah whisks kids away to Africa. Tours of the Amazon come through the eyes of the kids that live there. Visitors see the amazing things that are part of this area's residents' everyday world, just like the school bus is part of the world for kids in America. The pictures of these kids show what their lives are like. Does their skin or hair look different from kids' here? How about their clothes? Flipping through these pictures is like looking at a photo album from a faraway country.

Click the Tell Me About It! icon to learn about pictures on the site. Kids can learn that the oldest girl in one picture has to look after her little sisters while she tries to play, too. (Does that sound familiar?)

Take a break for a little fun with games like those in the Safari! section of the African tour. Mystery animals write poems that help kids guess their identities.

Fun facts and activities about the environment

National Wildlife Federation for Kids

http://www.nwf.org/kids

Wild America can be tough and strong, but the animals and land still need help from kids. That's why the National Wildlife Federation built this kids' Web site. Kids should stop here to learn what's best for wild animals and their environments. By doing so, they turn into real junior wildlife experts!

Cool Tours are a good way to start wildlife training. Journey through wetlands and public lands and learn about important topics such as endangered species and the water cycle. There are even cool experiments to try—like creating a water cycle at home. Kids can make a system that runs just like the rain and lakes in the real world. The tour ends when kids answer quiz questions about what they have just learned.

Lots of young wildlife fans read *Ranger Rick* magazine. Now, some the magazine is online. Rick's Homework section highlights Web sites that help kids with assignments.

Online Games lets kids match animal tracks with the animals themselves, such as coyote, muskrat, and chicken. Kids can act as meteorologists by building a rain gauge, or they can hunt for different plants and animals around town.

LINKS:
National Wildlife Federation, Take Action!

Walk the halls of an online nature museum

American Museum of Natural History

http://www.amnh.org

When it comes to history, we usually think about the things people have done. Most history classes cover important topics like wars, kings, and scientists. But the American Museum of Natural History shows that there's a lot more to history than just people. Studying natural history is all about learning the earth's life story. This museum in New York City is a fun place to do just that.

Anyone living near the museum can use the site to learn about its exhibits and plan a visit. Even for kids far from the museum, though, this Web site has plenty to see. The Explore section describes nature activities that kids ages 4 to 7 can do with their parents. Kids work just like real scientists on projects such as building a diorama (a scene or model) of a wading bird rookery or rain forest. Users test their observation skills by describing the differences between types of leaves.

The Electronic Newspaper has exciting articles about topics such as how museum workers put together dinosaur skeletons. The Sci-Q Quiz (in the Education section) tests kids' knowledge with questions about topics like the highest mountain on Earth and what living things are most numerous on the planet. (Hint: It's not people!)

Learn the history of the earth!

LINKS:
Young Naturalist Awards, Research, Imax Films

Take a make-believe trip

Disneyland

http://www2.disney.com/Disneyland/index.html

Disneyland is known as "the happiest place on Earth." It got its name from a marketing slogan, but kids and adults alike can't

Come see all your animated friends here.

help but have fun at this giant amusement park. The Disneyland Web site offers a fun tour of what's at the real Disneyland. Anyone planning to visit can use this site to figure out what to see when they arrive. And even folks who can't make it to Disneyland can take a pretend tour online.

Take a virtual tour of the park! Explore Disneyland has highlights of all the major park areas, including Frontierland, Fantasyland, and Critter Country. Kids learn about the rides and attractions, shops, and places to eat in each area.

The Business & Education section lists all sorts of special events that take place at Disneyland each year. Also check out the Art Lessons section. Kids might be able to talk their parents or teachers into letting them download the cool lessons to try at home.

In order to do this, kids will first have to download the Adobe Acrobat viewer program. The site supplies directions on how to obtain that free software.

LINKS:
Magic Music Days, Disneyland Today

Get up close and personal with ... dinosaurs

Children's Museum of Indianapolis Dinosaur Pages

http://www.childrensmuseum.org/kinetosaur/e.html

The pages in this Web site are like baseball cards of the biggest, scariest animals that ever lived. The Dinosaur Pages provide pictures of dinosaurs and throw in all the facts about each

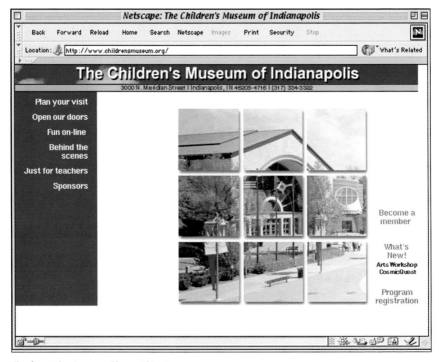

Check out the dinosaur files on this site.

animal. This site, from The Children's Museum of Indianapolis, is the perfect place to start any dinosaur research for school or just for fun.

Kids look through the list of dinosaur names and click an animal (such as Tyrannosaurus Rex). They'll see a color picture of the dinosaur pop up on the screen. All those teeth, claws, and horns add up to something *nobody* would want to mess with! Under the picture are all the facts about the dinosaur.

Kids can read about how big T. Rex and his dino buddies were and what they ate. T. Rex's teeth were each six inches long. Visitors should measure six inches on a ruler to get a better idea of the size of these monstrous creatures. Kids can click a link to print out a picture they can color. Anyone who colors enough pictures can start their own dinosaur hall of fame.

The FAQ (frequently asked questions) section answers common questions, such as "What is the largest known dinosaur?" and "How do dinosaurs get their names?" Once you check out the Dinosaur Pages, you'll be an expert among your friends!

Your computer can teach you about its own history

The Computer Museum

http://www.tcm.org/html/
galleries/network/index.html

Computers have sure changed since they were invented. Some of the first computers filled a whole room! A visit to The Computer Museum teaches interesting facts, such as how computers have gotten smaller as they've gotten more powerful. This site can help older kids learn about computers for school or just for fun.

The History button provides a quick computer history lesson. Every day, visitors learn different things about different computer events. The computer time line lists major events for each year.

However, this time line only goes up to 1990. That's ancient history in the computer world!

Real computer nuts should visit the Galleries for a detailed study of topics like Networks and Robots. These sections explain how computers around the world work together and how machines can do some of our work. A cool game lets kids work with friends on the Internet to put a picture together. It really shows what everyone can do with the right network. Many of the words in the articles can be clicked to reach more

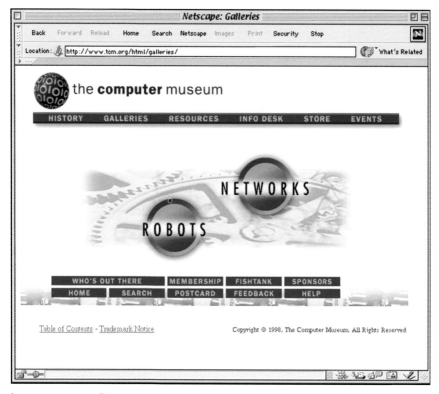

Let your computer tell its own story.

information (this feature is called "hypertext") so that users can study each topic as much as they want.

LINKS:

Kids & Computers, Careers in Computing, Computer Clubhouse

Visit a special museum page for kids

The Smithsonian Magazine Kids' Castle

http://www.kidscastle.si.edu

What can kids find when they dig through an old trunk full of stuff in Grandma's attic? There are probably all kinds of old-fashioned treasures. Imagine digging through the attic of our whole country! That's what visiting The Smithsonian Institution is like. This group of museums in Washington, D.C., collects everything from dinosaur bones to the first airplane.

On this site, you can check out the Smithsonian Institution magazine, *Kids' Castle,* written especially for young people. Here you can learn about science, the rest of the world, history, art, sports, animals, and other topics just by clicking on the icons on this home page. It's a really fun site.

There are also crafts projects, games, and lots of message boards for kids to have conversations about their favorite books, sports heroes, and entertainers!

LINK:
Smithsonian Magazine

Learn to cross virtual cultural boundaries

Culture Quest

http://www.ipl.org/youth/cquest/

Kids in faraway places such as Australia and Israel live a lot differently than Americans. Kids can find out just how different on a Culture Quest, where they try out life in other countries. Olivia Owl and Parsifal Penguin are ready to explain how all kinds of people live.

This trip with Olivia and Parsifal is a lot better than simply reading a book about other countries. These two birds show users what other countries are really like. For example, this site lists stories that kids in other lands hear before they go to bed. Greek kids hear the story about a wolf in sheep's clothing, just like the one lots of American kids are familiar with.

Kids in Israel eat foods like avocado with honey. This recipe, and many more, can be found on the site. Kids could surprise their class by bringing a foreign food to school the next time they have to bring treats. New games let users pretend they're kids in Brazil or another country. Brazilian kids love playing a game called Sick Cat. Would kids in American neighborhoods like it? Culture Quest is a big help for social studies classes, but it also shows that American kids aren't the only ones with great ideas for having a good time.

LINKS:
Internet Public Library Youth Page, Resources on Countries Visited

Tour the president's house with his cat and dog

The White House for Kids

http://www.whitehouse.gov/WH/ kids/html/home.html

The home of the president of the United States is no ordinary house, and the pet cat and dog living in the White House are no ordinary pets. Socks, President Clinton's cat, and Buddy, his dog, make great tour guides as they take kids on a trip through our country's most famous house. These animals share all the facts about the history and construction of the White House.

For instance, kids will learn that Washington, D.C. started as a big swamp with pigs roaming the streets. Kids see lots of pictures and learn about some adventurous moments in the White House halls, such as the time Dolly Madison rescued a painting of George Washington from a raging fire.

Buddy and Socks's tour gives kids a feel for what it's like to be a president's kid living in the White House. It's definitely not all business. Some of the jokes Abraham Lincoln's son Tad used to play were really mischievous! Of course, Socks and Buddy are fond of animals, so they share some pictures of White House pets such as Caroline Kennedy's pony (named Macaroni). Visitors see that animals play a big part in our nation's number-one home.

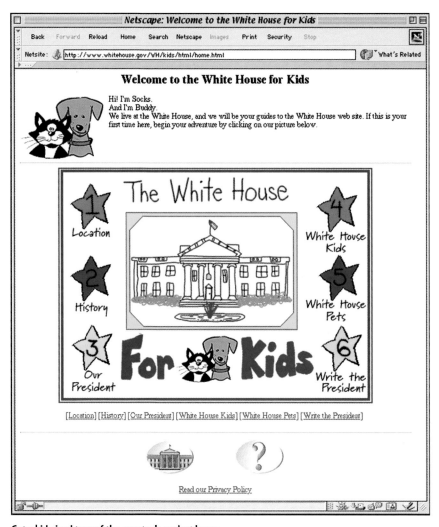

Get a kid-sized tour of the country's coolest house.

LINKS:
White House Kids, White House Pets, White House Home Page

Join the great explorers from the safety of your own home

Nationalgeographic.com/kids
http://www.nationalgeographic.com/kids

The world is pretty big, but the National Geographic Society staff has seen most of it. These adventurers travel the planet to check out amazing people, places, and animals. Anyone can see what they've been doing at National Geographic's online area for kids.

Read some amazing stories from *World* magazine for kids. There's even a story in the archives from one woman who rode on the *Titanic* when she was 12 (and survived). If you have something to say on any topic, get on the Kids Network to post your opinions for everyone else to read!

Have some fun with knowledge in the Fun & Games area. Laugh at the jokes and tongue twisters or test your brains with the GeoBee Challenge. (This contest uses real questions from the National Geography Bee.)

Older kids should be sure to visit Xpeditions. The area shows printable maps of almost any place on earth. It's great for school projects. A walk through the Xpedition Hall lets visitors run amazing machines, like the one that demonstrates ecosystems.

Check out what the world's greatest explorers are up to!

LINKS:
National Geographic Television, Geography Education, Cartoon Factory

Real-life adventures from around the world

The Discovery Channel

http://www.discovery.com/online.html

The best stories are about the real world that people live in. Everything—the oceans, the sky, the human body—holds exciting adventures. The Discovery Channel is a personal ticket to worlds most people have never seen.

A visit to the Feature Stories and Expeditions profiles people such as a businessman who's chasing the world's biggest floating ice cubes. He's capturing icebergs and melting them down to sell as drinking water!

Sometimes it seems like this Web site is actually part of the Discovery Channel on television. Pictures, videos, and audio clips make most of the stories come alive, so visitors won't just read about bear cubs, they'll hear them calling for their mom! The Animal Cams show pictures (taken just one minute earlier) of wild animals like sharks and cheetahs.

Share your opinions with other kids on topics in the Conversations area, or have fun with the three games offered at this site. There's something for everyone to enjoy, but good readers should get the most from the stories.

Come see the games, stories, and photos at this great site.

LINKS:

The Travel Channel, Discovery Channel School, The Learning Channel, Animal Planet

Chapter 5

Ideas for Real Life

There is a lot of information on the Web that can help kids have more fun or get great ideas for things to do. Kids can visit this section's sites, then turn off the computer and use their new ideas in real life. Some of these ideas can help people live longer and better, such as sites like Safety City and 10 Tips to Healthy Eating & Physical Activity.

Vince & Larry, the crash test dummies at Safety City, teach kids why they should wear seat belts. The 10 Tips site shows kids the benefits of eating healthy food—including vegetables—as well as their favorite stuff, such as pizza and ice cream.

Children will find instructions for some real hands-on projects hidden in a lot of these sites. A kid can start a career as a magician by learning simple magic tricks using objects around the house, or show artistic skills with a few craft projects. All kinds of hints and tips exist on the Web to help make kids' time *away* from the computer more fun and interesting.

Great activities for all types of weather

Summer Fun

http://www.netfix.com/poptart/summer.htm

Sometimes kids forget that summer's a time for having fun, not getting bored. It's no fun just sitting around watching television. The Summer Fun site can help get kids going with tons of great activity ideas. Some of the suggestions are for simple games to keep kids busy, but others describe awesome projects they can try.

Kids can get their hands dirty with a little gardening, for instance. The Garden Fun section tells kids how to grow all kinds of plants of their very own. Young gardeners can start little farms with lima bean sprouts, sweet potato vines, and carrots. Kids will even find instructions here for growing a house out of bean stalks! Using the recipes, kids can whip up some cool summer treats. It only takes graham crackers, bananas, and whipped cream to make delicious banana cream pies that kids can chomp in a few bites. Or they can try freezing some homemade popsicles.

When the weather turns nasty, check out the ideas in the Summer Fun's Indoor Fun section. Kids can ignore the bad weather with inside activities such as making watercolors from scratch, and then let their imaginations go with an afternoon of painting.

Tons of projects for kids of all ages

Making Friends

http://www.makingfriends.com

This site is so packed with crafts that kids can spend hours here. With instructions on everything from air fresheners to window watchers, kids are sure to find something to keep everyone happy and busy.

These crafts range in complexity, but most are fairly sophisticated. The listing on the crafts page rates the projects by grade level, so you can easily spot the ones that will work best for you. The projects are also grouped by theme, such as "Fun with Learning," "Preschool Paper Crafts," and "Gifts Kids can Make for Women," which is really helpful if you want the choice of several crafts. Each of the sections includes hints and tips to help with the projects.

> If you don't see a craft that you're looking for, or you're having trouble with a project you're working on, check out the bulletin board for ideas and advice. This is a very active message center for crafters, and you're sure to find new friends and get a helping hand.

Fans of Pikachu will be crazy about the crafts, with everything there to make a fun Pokémon party including a Pikachu piñata and party favors and a Pokémon trading card pouch.

Many of the crafts include templates that you can print out to get started, including patterns to make costumes and recipes to make gooey mixtures like "Flubber." For more complicated crafts, step-by-step instructions are illustrated. If you are *really* inspired by the crafts, the site also features lots of books and supplies that you can buy online.

LINKS:
Crafts, Forum, Contest

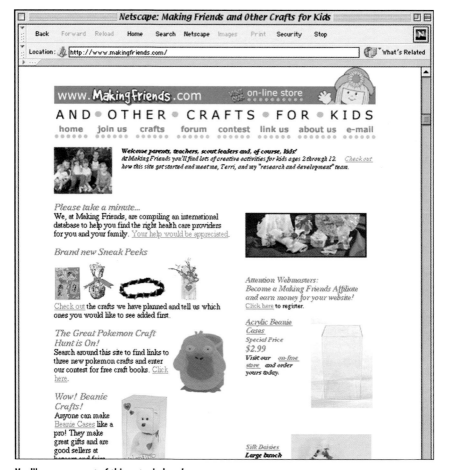

You'll never run out of things to do here!

Great ideas for turning castoffs into treasures

Kids' Domain Craft Exchange—Crafts From Recycled Materials

http://www.kidsdomain.com/craft/_recycle.html

Don't throw away those old broken crayons, Band-Aid boxes, or pasta boxes. They can come to life again as candles, pencil holders, or picture frames. With a little bit of skill and a lot of imagination, you can use common household items to create beautiful projects to give as gifts or to keep for yourself!

There are instructions here for dozens of crafts that use things from around the house (like old Styrofoam meat trays), so you don't have to go out and buy a lot of stuff to get started.

> If you want to get outside and do a creative project, go to the link for projects by natural materials. Here you'll find crafts that use stuff from the backyard, such as acorns, bark, and leaves. You can create masterpieces including pebble pets, pinecone wreaths, and rock paperweights.

The page also includes a helpful link to projects by material, so if you have lots of old cans lying around that you don't know what to do with, just click "cans and jars" and you'll find more projects. There are also lists of projects that use boxes, tubes, and fabric.

The projects range from "very easy" to "average," but most of the crafts are rated "easy" and don't require much skill or many tools. Each craft lists all the ingredients you'll need, along with step-by-step instructions. Some of the crafts also include instructions for variations on the project, and tips from people who have made the craft.

The more difficult crafts, especially the ones that require lots of cutting, will require help from grown-ups.

LINKS:
KD Review, Downloads, Grownups Place

Get great ideas for crafts at this site.

Write songs and make music with everyday objects

Pipsqueaks

http://www.childrensmusic.org/Pipsqueaks.html

Music is a big part of life. A good tune can help everybody—from little kids to adults—get through the day with a smile. Imagine how boring the radio or movies would be without music!

That's never a problem at the Pipsqueaks site. Its musical goodies will keep kids' toes tapping wherever they go. The main idea at Pipsqueaks is to have fun with music. Try singing along with audio clips of silly songs written by other kids. Some first graders wrote a funny song about Elvis the butterfly. Listen to it, then jump over to the Tall and Small Reviews to see what other kids and adults think of the same music. Kids can play radio star by recording their own radio program. Pipsqueaks tells kids how to set up a recording studio in a closet and how to make cool sound effects for the show.

One great thing about music is that anybody can play it, even if they can't play the piano or guitar. The Create section shows kids that anything can make sounds, even comb and paper or their own heartbeats. Artis the Spoonman and other musicians give kids lessons in playing common objects like teaspoons.

LINKS:
Children's Music Web, Kids' Radio, Hand Jive

Learn to live healthy–and have fun doing it

10 Tips to Healthy Eating & Physical Activity

http://ificinfo.health.org/brochure/10tipkid.htm

Kids shouldn't mistreat their bodies! It's important for kids to lead healthy lives, just as it is for adults. When kids keep their bodies happy, they'll feel better. It's easy for kids to treat their bodies right with the 10 Tips to Healthy Eating & Physical Activity.

These ideas tell a young person just what to do in order to make their body a high-performance machine. These tips will really benefit kids who are willing to work a little. The tips include suggestions like starting each day with a good, healthy breakfast so the body's engine has fuel to run. Other helpful tips cover exercise pointers, such as joining in during physical education classes at school or playing sports to get good work-outs. Each tip helps kids get started by suggesting foods that are good for them and that taste great, such as bagels and spaghetti.

Kids can also take a trip to the Food Guide Pyramid by clicking on its link. There they will be able to see more secrets of healthy kids. This table shows kids how much of each type of food to eat every day.

Drop into the Cafe to cook up some tasty fun

CafeZOOM

http://www.pbs.org/wgbh/zoom/cafe

Aspiring chefs will have a tasty time in CafeZOOM, the place to go to make all the recipes you see featured on Zoom, the popular PBS kids' show.

The recipes are easy to make, some with just a few ingredients, and many don't even involve using the stove. Take the Peanut Butter Treats, for instance, which 53.9 percent of ZOOMers call "heavenly." All you need is peanut butter, vanilla, honey, and instant milk (and a little chocolate topping, of course). Just mix, roll, and cool, and you've made yourself a fantastic, tasty snack. You barely need a grown-up at all (but make sure you ask permission first).

Though there are lots of snacks, there are also some great lunch ideas featured, including tortilla sandwiches and pizza bagels. New recipes are added all the time. Recipes are rated, too, so you can see what real kids think.

> If you want to print out your favorite recipes from CafeZOOM, click on the "text-only" button, which will take out the fancy pictures and leave you with an easy-to-print version. You may want to print them all and create your own Zoom cookbook!

You can even add your own two cents. If you have a recipe that you

Come on and zoom, zoom, zoom-a-zoom!

think is worthy of the CafeZOOM, send it in. If it passes the Zoom tasters, you might see it featured on the show and at the Cafe!

LINKS:
Zoinks, ZOOMtoo, Some Stuff

Get down and dirty with these fun science activities

Ooey, Gooey Recipes for the Classroom

http://www.minnetonka.k12.mn.us/support/ science/tools/ooey.html

Slimy, wet, and sticky—that's how you'd describe the projects on this page. These fun science activities are definitely for days when you're ready to get your hands and your clothes dirty.

The recipes, which are compiled from the Minnetonka Elementary Science Center, include finger paint, several varieties of slime, gak, Play-doh, and silly putty. Though the site says these are projects for the classroom, they're also a blast at home.

> For a real science lesson, check out the recipe for PVA slime. The project uses polyvinyl alcohol (PVA) and Borax to create a strong slimelike gel. The recipe includes an in-depth, scientific explanation of the separate elements, and suggests lots of questions for kids to consider as they make (and play with) slime.

There are lots of recipes for bubbles—big bubbles, tough bubbles, and bubbles within bubbles. And if making bubbles is not enough, you can learn all about the physics of bubbles, too. You'll learn how bubbles are formed, how soap makes them stronger, and why rainbows of colors swirl in bubbles.

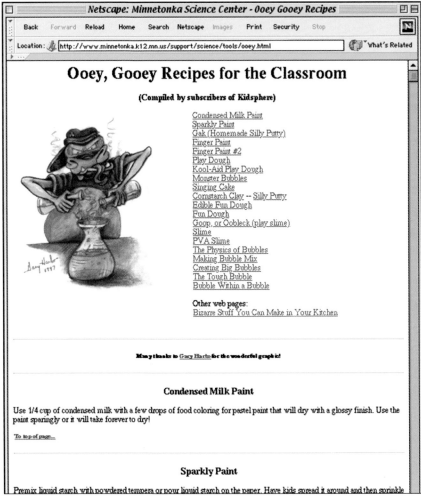

Learn to do gross but fun science experiments!

If you really want to be the life of the party, try the singing cake recipe! You heard that right: Using a combination of baking powder, buttermilk, egg yolks, and more, you can make a cake that sings as it bakes. Since the recipe also calls for chocolate, sugar, and strawberry jam, the cake is also delicious to eat once the song is done!

Learn safety smarts from a pair of famous dummies

Safety City

http://www.nhtsa.dot.gov/kids

Vince and Larry know a lot about being unsafe. In fact, their job is to have bad accidents every day. But these crash test dummies are glad to do it. Through their work, Vince and Larry learn safety tips that they can then pass on to kids (and adults). Learn from all their wrecks by reading their safety advice on the Web.

The crash test dummies are famous for their car wrecks and seat belt safety, but they can teach kids to be safe in a lot of different ways. Kids can click Safety School to learn lessons on avoiding injuries. The Safety Challenge tests how much kids know and shows what they need to study. The Bike Tour button teaches pedal-pushers really important biking tips. Vince and Larry help kids learn how to check their bike equipment, how to ride correctly around cars, and how to watch out for danger zones around town.

Vince and Larry have been in more than 10,000 crashes in the Research Lab. Read about what happens to people in car crashes and how seat belts can save lives. Then kids will see why only real dummies don't buckle up.

LINKS:
National Highway Traffic Safety Administration, Theater, School Bus

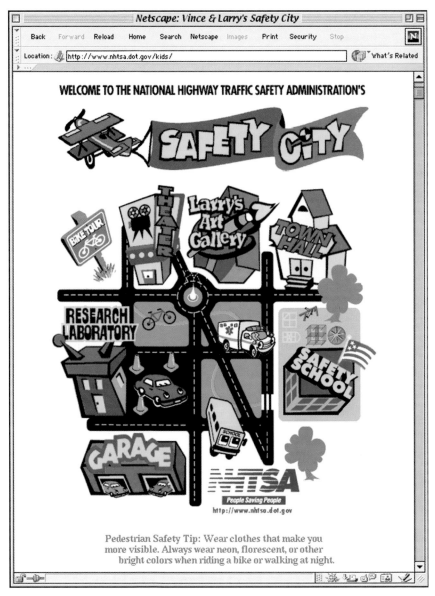

This cool site is full of fun stuff about staying safe.

Become a magician by learning some simple tricks

Conjuror–Magic Tricks

http://www.conjuror.com/magictricks

Magic tricks are amazing to watch. How can a magician tie a knot in a handkerchief with one hand? Kids can learn the secrets to this trick, and others, at the Conjuror site. They'll

Presto–change-o! It's a cool magic site!

see that magic tricks don't require special powers. Each budding magician just has to practice their tricks until they get good enough to fool their friends.

The Conjuror site teaches 15 magic tricks designed for beginners. Each uses items commonly found around the house, such as coins and string. That means kids don't have to worry about finding someone to saw in half! Be sure to ask Mom or Dad before trying these tricks. Some use matches or other items that can be dangerous.

Clear explanations teach kids how to do each trick, and pictures show them how to do each move. Older kids can tackle some of the harder tricks, such as the ones using several piles of playing cards. Pay attention to the instructions that tell which card goes where!

Younger kids will also find tricks they can try, like the trick of the magnetic butter knife. Kids who decide to become master magicians can use the site's links to learn more. The links point kids to advanced tricks and stores that sell magic supplies.

There is also a cool mailing list you can subscribe to, as well as an online history of magic. Here, you can read about how people viewed magic hundreds of years ago, as well as about Harry Houdini and the story of juggling.

Here's how kids can help the planet

Earth Force

http://www.earthforce.org/welcome.htm

Don't just talk about helping the environment. *Do* something about it! The earth is the only place we live, so we'd better keep it nice. There are a lot of ways kids can improve water quality, wildlife habitats, and other environmental situations in their own towns. The Earth Force page tells you how to make a difference.

Start with the Take Action button. It describes things that kids can do to help the planet, such as riding a bike instead of asking their parents to drive them. Easy transportation alternatives like this can help cut down on air pollution. Kids can also find places in their town to plant new trees, then they can call up a community tree specialist who can get them planted.

Earth Force helps children understand what the big environmental problems are. This site shows that a lot of our streams are filled with bad chemicals called pollutants. Kids might be able to start a project in their neighborhood to decrease existing water pollution. Kids who do something to help raise awareness of environmental issues should write to Earth Force about it. The folks at Earth Force love to hear how kids are making things happen.

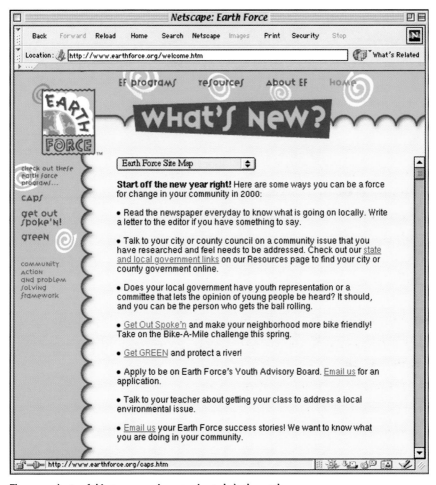

There are plenty of things you can do every day to help the earth.

Save a few bucks and order some free stuff

Absolutely Free Stuff for Kids and Parents

http://www.ppi-free.com/freekid.htm

It's great to get something for nothing. It's also fun to get something in the mail. At Absolutely Free Stuff for Kids and Parents, both can happen. This big list tells kids how to order everything from information booklets to craft kits to packages of games. Just write to the mailing addresses listed on the site. It might cost a couple of dollars for shipping and handling, but kids can get a lot of neat items without spending their whole allowance.

A lot of the giveaways are booklets for kids. Send away for the "Billy Buck Hightrail's Secret Mysterious Magical Garden" booklet to learn about eating the right foods. Other booklets help kids decide what to be when they grow up. Send in for free copies of kids' magazines such as *The Turtle* and *Jack & Jill*. Kids can order tons of free craft kits here. Some are patterns that help children make neat toys, such as a bottle cap yo-yo. Other free kits have everything kids will need to make crafts such as a finger-size mouse puppet or a stuffed penguin toy. Click the link to the free catalogs section to order catalogs for all kinds of neat stuff.

Here's a place to score some cool stuff for nothing!

LINKS:
Free Stuff Newsletter!, How to Suggest a Free Offer, Free Stuff for Sewing

Kids can learn to do almost anything

Learn2.com

http://www.learn2.com

It can be really embarrassing for kids if they don't know how to make their bed, iron clothes, research family history, or even shoot a free throw. Kids can ask their parents or (oh no!) even their older brothers or sisters to show them, but that can be embarrassing too. Some kids just want to learn how to do things all by themselves.

That's where Learn2.com can help. Kids can stop here to "learn 2" do almost anything, including all the little things they've never quite figured out. It's a perfect site for curious, computer-literate kids.

Start by clicking Search. Kids can type in "make a bed," for example, and get instructions for making their bed perfectly. That'll impress their parents! Kids will learn to do each thing using the easy instructions and pictures that show them exactly what to do. This makes it easy for kids to learn something as difficult as making their own writing paper.

While kids are studying one task, Learn2.com suggests other things to learn. That way kids get smarter every time they visit. Although Learn2.com is a great place to figure out how to do school projects, chores, and other "responsible stuff," be sure

Just ask for help, and you'll get it.

to learn about things other than the boring stuff kids *have* to do. Learn2.com also teaches kids how to do fun activities like making your own jigsaw puzzle or playing checkers.

LINKS:
2torial Top 10, Learnlines

Learn safety rules from real police officers

Kid Safety on the Internet

http://www.ou.edu/oupd/kidsafe/start.htm

The world can seem pretty scary when kids think about all the ways they could run into trouble at school, on the sidewalk, or even online. But if children learn safety rules for all these places, they don't have to be afraid. Police officers have filled the Kid Safety on the Internet site with tips to make sure kids are safe.

Click the Kid Safety button to open a slide show. Click the big arrow buttons at the bottom of the screen to turn the pages in the police officer's notebook and see the next picture. The first screen gives kids basic rules for being safe online, such as being careful about talking to strangers. Other slide show pages quiz kids' safety knowledge with questions such as "Do you know what to do after an accident?" The answers are always found right on the next page. Some examples of other safety tips are what to do when a kid meets strange animals, rides a bike, or faces a bully.

When finished with the Kid Safety section, check out the site's main page. The police provide great tips for topics that include kitchen safety and recognizing poisonous plants. Kids should get Mom and Dad to explore the site with them so that everyone can learn how to be safer.

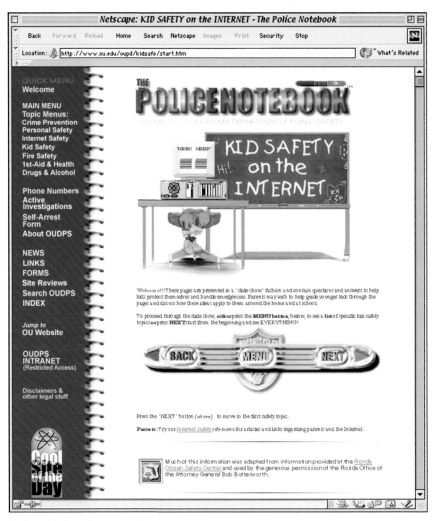

Explore *this* site with your whole family.

Chapter 6

Names You Know

Moving to a new place, whether it's a whole new town or just a new school, is tough. That's one problem kids won't have when they start exploring the Web. The online world might be new, but many of the faces on the Web are familiar.

Lots of the sites in the Names You Know section let fans get to know their favorite stars from sports, music, and movies a little bit better. Star Seeker, for example, has photos and facts about superstars such as Sammy Sosa, Britney Spears, and Jim Carrey.

Two other names kids already know are LEGO and Crayola. These building blocks and crayons have been coloring kids' imaginations for years. Now kids can see LEGO creations, tour a crayon factory, and develop ideas galore while visiting these Web pages.

Some of these sites really let kids get involved with the stars. Dr. Seuss has been famous for a long time for his funny books, but his Web site even includes some new video games that let players team up with characters from his books!

Answers to science questions and fun experiments to try

You Can with Beakman & Jax

http://www.beakman.com

Beakman knows that science and a good time can go together. On TV, *Beakman's World* is packed with wacky science lessons and experiments, and the Beakman Web site is just as good. It's based on the *You Can with Beakman & Jax* cartoon strip, which runs in newspapers. The Web site has the answers to science questions that kids might ask, such as "How does soap work?" Plus it lets everybody dig into science projects with demonstrations for kids to try.

Beakman's main feature is the answers to the 50 most frequently asked science questions. Beakman gives the lowdown on interesting questions such as "Where do dreams come from?" After each answer, he describes a related experiment kids can try. One experiment teaches kids how to dream in a certain color! Nobody gets bored reading about *these* science topics.

The Interactive Demos are moving pictures that show how different aspects of science work. Animations illustrate a lot of neat functions, such as blood flowing in the body or tiny particles in metal shifting due to magnetic attraction. Science really makes sense when Beakman explains the ideas. No wonder he's famous for making science fun!

Is the force with you?

Rebel Friends

http://www.theforce.net/kids

Now you can join forces with characters from the original and the prequel Star Wars series. By visiting nine planets from a galaxy far, far away, you can choose what type of activity you

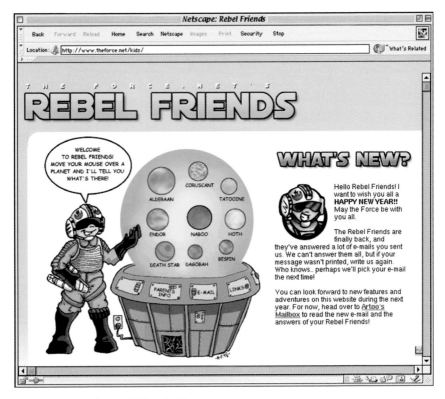

Go from planet to planet with the rebels!

want to do. You'll find adventures even greater than what you see in the movies!

A different Star Wars character acts as your host on each planet. Luke Skywalker will take you back in time on the planet Tatooine, where you'll meet the young Anakin Skywalker. Together, you can solve the mystery of a large ship that has landed on the planet. This interactive game lets you choose the next move, whether it's staying in bed because it's too cold outside or talking with Watto, a junkyard owner. You're in for a big surprise when you figure out who the mysterious ship belongs to!

Jedi wannabes can visit Coruscant to see if they have what it takes to become a Jedi, and fans of Jar Jar Binks will want to help him locate stolen Bunny Bunny eggs on the beautiful planet of Naboo. On the Death Star, Darth Vader is the anchor of Vader's News Network (VNN), a show that runs nonstop Dark Side propaganda.

You may choose to travel to Alderaan, where Princess Leia will take you to the Museum of Beautiful Artwork. You'll find pictures of all your favorite Star Wars characters to print out and color, and you can also view drawings submitted by kids just like you. You can even send in your own pictures; perhaps *your* artwork will be posted! Kids e-mail questions are answered here, too!

Building blocks for kids' imaginations

LEGO Worlds

http://www.lego.com/worlds.asp

Anyone who can snap two blocks together and dream up big ideas can build almost anything with LEGO blocks. Millions of these famous plastic blocks go into kids' projects around the world. But snappable blocks are just the beginning of the amazing building tools described at the LEGO Worlds Web site.

On the main page, kids can click on a diverse and always-changing assortment of LEGO themes. Clicking one of the theme pictures provides information about what's available from LEGO in that area. This is a great way to see what's new in favorite toys. Some areas have special features such as digital postcards kids can send that have pictures of LEGO toys. The sites are updated monthly, so there's always something cool to do!

The New on www.lego.com button is the quickest path to the best entertainment LEGO offers online. Items listed here include cool adventure games and interactive stories. On the Internet, LEGO has a lot of great ideas besides little blocks!

Hang around LEGOland for a while!

Science facts and experiments for kids

Nye Labs Online

http://nyelabs.kcts.org

It seems safe to take science lessons from somebody called "The Science Guy." That's why so many kids turn to Bill Nye, the "official" TV Science Guy, to learn how things work and why things happen. Bill's lab is open to online visitors any time. The sites on this tour just might make science everybody's new favorite subject.

The Demo Of The Day is the place to look for Bill's tips on demonstrations designed for young scientists. Tips explain experiments such as using food coloring to show how flowers drink water. Kids can check the Demo every day to build their own series of scientific explorations.

The TV Guide tells a little about the next show's topic and points out where and when you can catch a rerun of your favorite episode. When Bill can't cover everything about a subject, he'll suggest places to get more information. The Teacher's Lounge button points to related sites that he recommends.

The Goodies button has a collection of fun stuff, like Bill Nye's photo album and the Video Clips screening room, which has video clips of Bill in action. Sounds Of Science lets everybody listen to sound clips from episodes of *Bill Nye the Science Guy.*

Get tips from the pros

Baseball for Kids

http://www.majorleaguebaseball.com/ u/kids/mlbcom/kids

Play ball! Kids hanging around this site feel almost like pro baseball players. It offers an inside look at life as a big-league hitter, a star pitcher, or even as one of the behind-the-scenes folks who make baseball games possible.

The stories here show that big-time baseball stars are real people too. What do big leaguers do when they're not playing baseball? Some like to fish and golf, while others like to surf the Web—just like you! This site changes often, so you can read new stories about star players all the time.

The pros at this site are ready to share tips on secrets of the game. Instructions explain the best way to break in a new glove. Kids can also get pointers on improving their fielding and hitting skills from current star players. Users learn that it's important to do proper stretching and warm-up exercises, too.

Pro baseball involves more than just players and coaches. Stories here show that the cleanup crews, ushers, and other folks work as hard as the players do to make sure that every baseball game is a good one.

Get up close and personal with the Hogwarts gang

Meet Harry Potter

http://www.scholastic.com/harrypotter

Do the names Hermione Granger, Ron Weasly, and Draco Malfoy mean anything to you? If you're like most kids, you need no introduction to the gang from the Hogwarts School for Witchcraft and Wizardry.

Fans (and fanatics) of the entrancing Harry Potter books will be bewitched by this site, which is full of games, quizzes, interviews, and discussions on all the books in the *Harry Potter* series.

For each book, there is a sample chapter to read and games to test your knowledge (for example, do you remember who took Harry shopping for school supplies his first year?). Kids who want to go behind the scenes with Harry will love the interview with author J. K. Rowling, who fills kids in on the little tidbits about writing the book—like how she came up with the names for her characters (for instance, dumbledore is an old English word for bumble bee), where she writes her books, and her plans for future books in the series.

> Harry Potter fans can hook up with fans from around the world to share their opinions in the "Reading Circle." Fans talk about their favorite characters in the book and give details on what made the character come alive for them and how that character compares to Harry.

More info about the world's most popular kids' books.

Think you know everything there is to know about Harry Potter? Print out the crossword puzzle and try to figure out the clues about the first three books. For another challenge, unscramble the words in the Wizard Words game.

LINKS:
Discussion Guides, Harry Potter Screen Saver, Read what they're saying about Harry

A visit to the cyberhome of Steve and Blue

Blue's Clues

http://www.nickjr.com/bluesclues/home.html

Join Steve, Blue, Magenta, and the rest of the *Blue's Clues* gang for more fun at their online home, which is packed with games, activities, and a behind-the-scenes look at the show.

You've got all the clues to find online fun here!

Kids who want to bring the fun of the show back to their own house should click on the picture frame on the wall, where they will find lots of fun activities. Kids can print out some pages to color, listen to Blue's birthday song, or even download an autographed picture of Steve and Blue.

> If you have questions about Blue's Clues, this is the place to come for answers. Why do they repeat the show every day for a week? Does Steve ever change his clothes? Is Blue a boy or a girl? Cruise around and you'll find the answers.

If you want to know what's cooking, check out Blue's recipes, where you'll learn how to make some of the cool food you see on the show (including banana muffins and orange juice pops). There are also step-by-step directions on how to make some of the crafts from the show so you can try them out for yourself.

For every episode, you can keep the fun rolling by downloading a game from the site. There's a new game for each episode, and each one reinforces the theme of that show. In the cash register game, for example, kids learn about counting, addition, and subtraction as they use their money to buy things at a store. Other games teach sorting, matching, and shapes.

LINKS:
Steve's Page, News and Boutique, Sounds and Pictures

Your ticket to Nick news, games, and more

Nickelodeon

http://www.nick.com

The TV show listings at the Nickelodeon site are pretty handy. They help kids find out when their favorite programs come on so they don't miss an episode. But Nickelodeon's site has so much to do that kids just might forget about turning on the TV.

A backstage tour with Inside Nick shows what goes on behind the cameras. It's the place to get to know all the big Nick stars a little better. This inside knowledge comes from people who ought to know, such as the moms of Nick stars. They share secrets about what their kids like to eat and whether they clean their rooms. Splat! has answers to the most outrageous questions sent in by kids visiting the site. Information here is updated weekly and includes fun facts such as what junk food the stars eat while they're working. An artist even shows how he draws CatDog, giving step-by-step instructions.

Nick's games are some of the best on the Web, and they are updated often. Creepy kids can compose their own ghoulish tunes with the Music Decomposer. And kids' ability to observe a situation closely is tested by Harriet the Spy. Easy instructions explain how to download each game.

LINKS:
Write to Nick, Nick at Nite, Nick Jr.

Join your favorite tug in his next adventure

Theodore Tugboat Online Activity Centre

http://www.pbs.org/tugboat/activities/index.html

Theodore Tugboat is a strong little boat that can handle tough jobs around the harbor. But this TV star needs help with his latest adventure on the Web.

Should he make friends with the new ship in the harbor or should he see what his jobs for the day will be? Talk to Barrington Barge? Head home or listen to a story? Readers can decide what he'll do next in the interactive stories at Theodore's Web site. Kids can read a few lines in a story, then click a link to decide Theodore's next move. The rest of the story depends on what kids choose, so they'd better give Theodore good advice!

All those decisions can be tough. When it's time to relax, there's a link to listen to a Theodore story. A friendly voice tells exciting stories, such as one about the day a storm blew away Kulu the Canoe and Theodore had to rescue him. There's a new story every month. (Users need the special RealAudio tool to listen to these stories; a link tells how to download it for free.)

Theodore's online coloring book lets kids print out pictures of this super little boat. Kids can color the pictures and make up their own Theodore stories.

A super collection of famous comics–updated daily

Comics.com

http://www.unitedmedia.com/comics

Comic strip characters may be just funny little drawings, but they're smart enough to hang out where all their fans can see them. Comics.com is the place where some of the most famous newspaper cartoon characters make their Web home. Most newspapers don't include all of these comics, but the Web hangout features popular strips such as *Luann, Marmaduke, Dilbert, Herman, Frank & Ernest,* and many more.

Visitors can pick a strip's name from the comic list at the top of the page and dig into the funnies online.

The *Peanuts* area by itself is worth the visit. It features information on the history of the strip, profiles of characters and the artist, digital postcards, crossword puzzles, and word games. The Timeline is an interesting way to learn about *Peanuts.* Visitors can click any date to see what Snoopy and the gang were up to at that time. When this comic strip got started way back in 1950, Snoopy looked really different!

Editoons includes political cartoons that use pictures to talk about the news. In the United Media Store, kids can buy stuff (with their parents' permission) that features favorite characters including Luann T-shirts, *Peanuts* books, and Dilbert dolls.

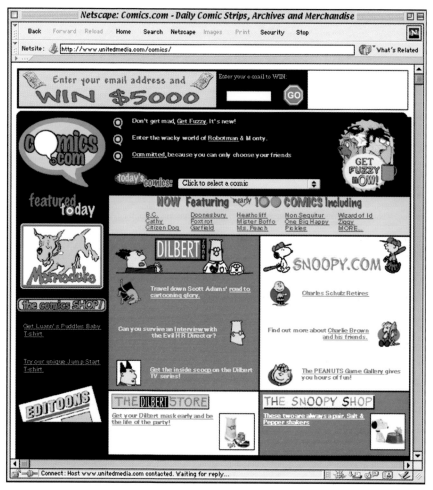

They may just be cartoons, but they sure do get around on the net!

Find information on celebrities, pop stars, and sports heroes here

Star Seeker

http://www.starseeker.com

Michael Jordan's here. So is Hanson. Even Will Smith's here. In fact, this fan site is the place to check up on all your favorite sports heroes, movie stars, and entertainers. Fans can even find out about the movies, TV shows, and albums themselves. The people running Star Seeker make sure that only the top celebrity links get in. That way this site always has the best available resources for news, photos, and cool information about the stars.

The main page makes it easy to find a favorite star. Star Seeker sorts sites into easy-to-use categories such as Music, TV, Movies, Movie Stars & Other Celebs, and Sports. Finding a star is as easy as clicking one of these categories and then choosing other categories to find the right topic. Kids can click Movie Stars & Other Celebs, for example, then click Cartoons. They'll see listings of sites for all kinds of cartoon heroes, including Batman, Garfield, Popeye, and the X-Men.

The categories let fans quickly find just the right information. If a fan wants to know when their favorite band's next album will come out, they can use the Music section to find sites about groups like Hanson, the Spice Girls, or the Backstreet Boys.

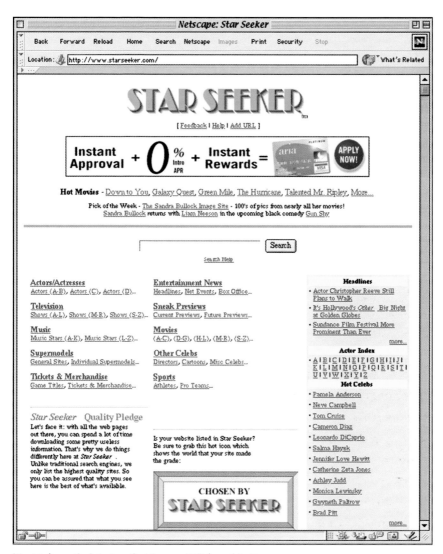

Want to know the latest on the big names? Click on this site.

LINKS:
Hot Movies, Pick of the Week

The best of great kids' TV on the net

PBS Kids!

http://www.pbs.org/kids

Television fans can visit Mister Rogers' Neighborhood, plus Sesame Street, Teletubbies country, and Wimzie's House all at the same place: They share an address at PBS Kids Online. This site helps kids learn more about all their favorite PBS

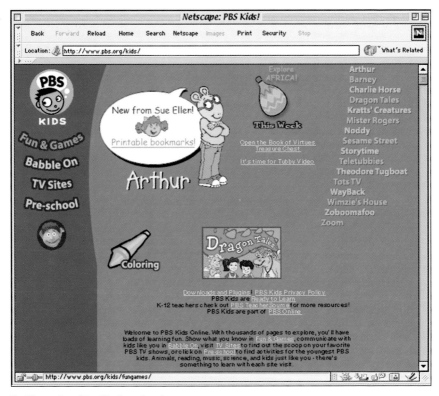

You'll see a lot of familiar faces here!

(which stands for Public Broadcasting System) shows. With so much to do and see, this site might be even more fun than watching the shows on TV.

The main PBS site serves up a whole grab bag of fun activities. The Fun & Games link points to the games. Kid Karaoke, which you can get to by clicking on Pre-School, is one of the best features of the PBS site. This online jukebox plays music and displays the words to songs on the screen. Young singers can sing along as long as they want. The Babble On link allows kids to voice their opinions in polls or share their thoughts by writing to their favorite PBS characters.

One PBS favorite that you can learn all about is Arthur the Aardvark. He and his sister D.W. are always up to something, and you can catch up to them here.

Sections for the shows help viewers enjoy each program more. For example, the area on *Mister Rogers' Neighborhood* explains activities kids can try that match his topics each day.

LINKS:
Charlie Horse Music Pizza, Storytime, Tots TV

Sam-I-Am and Horton want visitors

Seussville

http://www.randomhouse.com/seussville

Even people who hate green eggs and ham will like Dr. Seuss' home on the Web. Funny characters such as Horton and the Lorax are running around his site to make sure everyone has a good time. The games and other activities are just as much fun as the Dr. Seuss books the world loves to read.

Then it's time to play along with Dr. Seuss characters in the Games area. There's a whole group of games that require the special Shockwave browser plug-in. Onscreen instructions show how to download the special tool. Then kids can try to shoot a hoop in Elephant Ball or fix a picture in the Green Eggs and Ham Picture Scramble. Digging out a pencil gets players ready for the special collection of games that can be printed out and played on paper, including a maze that winds through the Cat's famous hat.

There's a daily dose of wacky, wise advice in the More Fun section's daily Seussisms. Kids can also test how well they know Seuss books with the Trivia Contest. For example, where does Thidwick the Big-Hearted Moose live? If that sounds too hard, kids can relax and follow the coloring instructions for making their own Many Colored Bookmark.

They got game! Dribble to the online home of the WNBA

WNBA

http://www.wnba.com

Women playing pro basketball can pop the trey or take it to the rim, and fans learn all about it at the WNBA's official Web site. It's *the* spot to check scores and highlights and find out what life is like for these world-class athletes.

The site has lots of videos of great WNBA action. Highlights spotlight great game moments, such as some great shots from way outside and a big block from Malgorzata Dydek, who is 7'2" tall. Special audio clips demonstrate that these women have talent off the court, too. One clip shows a few stars singing in the WNBA's "Join In" TV commercial.

The Interactive section is the place to join chat sessions with WNBA stars. Fans can even vote for their own WNBA All-Star team. A special Players section helps everybody get to know the athletes. Kids can find out that Rebecca Lobo likes Road Runner cartoons and that she once went jogging with the President of the United States!

And if kids start itching to get active during their visit, the WNBA players always have some tips on how young athletes can learn to keep in shape.

LINKS:
Teams, NBA.com, Season Schedule

The hot spot to get and share video game tips

KidsCom GamePad

http://www.kidscom.com/orakc/gamepad/index.shtml

If you're crazy about video games, you can find plenty of places to buy and sell cartridges and other equipment on the Internet. But to get *good* at your favorite games, the place to go is Kids Com GamePad.

At this great site, kids can learn about mastering their favorite games—but they also learn how to reason, think deductively, and look for clues.

GamePad offers help on games for Nintendo 64, GameBoy, Sega Genesis and Saturn, PlayStation, and a lot more. A Tip of the Week tells how to earn extra points, solve tough problems, or use codes to reveal secrets hidden in all the hottest games.

The More Tips link includes a whole collection of tricks. Smart gamers drop in on the Game Talk message boards to ask game questions and give advice.

Hotshot players can take the KidsCom Challenge. GamePad shows a tough spot in a game and challenges players to send in their best strategies for getting past it. One challenge asks kids to make Yoshi celebrate in front of a melon (instead of a big heart) in "Yoshi's Story." Correct answers go into a drawing for special KidsKash Points that help winners earn prizes.

If you're hungry for video game info, check this site out.

LINKS:

KidsCom Main Site, Make New Friends, Cool Stuff

Get creative coloring ideas

Crayola

http://www.crayola.com/

Everybody knows a lot about Crayola crayons. After all, average kids in North America use up to 730 crayons by the time they are ten years old! That's just one of the neat facts found at the Crayola site.

Why not start with finding out how crayons get here in the first place? A tour of the factory shows how markers and crayons

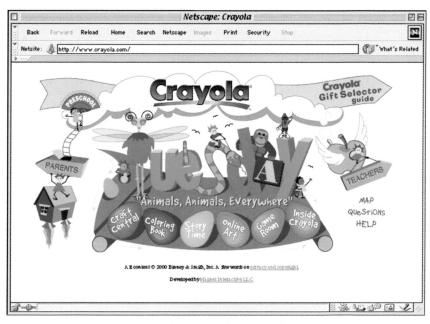

You've used crayons on paper. Now see how they look on the Web!

are made. Those giant barrels of wax in the picture are moved through the plant and eventually become crayons. The Fun Facts section has trivia teasers on topics such as which two crayon colors are kids' favorites. The Colorful History link provides visitors with the story of Crayola crayons. For instance, in 1903, there were only eight colors!

From the Coloring Book, kids can print fun pictures to color. And if kids are looking for some creative coloring ideas, the Idea Generator is just the ticket. This section helps kids come up with some really kooky coloring topics!

If you want to play some coloring or matching games, or solve some puzzles, be sure to hit the Game Room. Here, you can try your hand at games for "beginners" or "old pros."

This site is not *just* about crayons. In the Craft section, kids can choose a new project to work on each week. Kids who have cool craft ideas can send them to Crayola. Who knows? Maybe their ideas will be added to this site's craft collection!

LINKS:
Crayola FamilyPlay, Tools for Fun, Scavenger Hunt

Bunches of Beanies for fans and collectors

The Official Home of the Beanie Babies

http://www.beaniebabies.com

Everybody wants to get their hands on Beanie Babies. For the official news on Beanie Babies, come to the site posted by their maker, Ty, Inc., at The Official Home of the Beanie Babies.

When fans are looking for the scoop on new Beanies, checking out what's missing from their collections, or just looking to talk with other collectors, they'll find what they need at this site. The Beanie Babies Collection page gives the name and picture of every animal. All of the cute, cuddly collectibles are here, from Erin the bear to Web the spider.

These online Beanies aren't just ordinary toys. Some of the animals keep diaries and put them on the Web site. Kids can read about how the Beanies keep busy every day doing things like playing games and visiting friends.

Anyone can sign up for a free Beanie Connection membership and share messages with other fans. Members can talk about everything "Beanie," including what price is right for a new addition to their collection or what their favorite Beanie is and why.

LINKS:
Beanie Babies Official Club, Beanie Connection

An ideal site to keep young readers turning the pages

Just for Kids Who Love Books

http://www3.sympatico.ca/alanbrown/kids.htm

Scary books, country books, animal books, fairy tale books—they're all covered here at a site that helps kids find out more about their favorite books. A friendly librarian from Canada built this site to help young readers. The big list of links points to sites about great kids' books all over the World Wide Web.

The left side of the screen holds all the links, which list names of authors, titles of books, and names of book series. Visiting a site about a favorite author or book is as easy as clicking. Book links include titles from series such as *The Baby-Sitters Club,* the *Little House* books, *Goosebumps,* and *Winnie The Pooh.*

The site for every book is different, so exploring a lot of them doesn't get boring. Most of the sites include pictures, such as those from the "Goosebumps" television show. Other sites list all the books written by a specific author. This helps fans of certain authors decide what book to read next. Sometimes a book site has audio and video clips. All these links are great ways for kids to get more fun out of the books they like to read.

LINKS:
Authors, Titles and Series

Chapter 7

Multimedia Resources

It's a movie screen. It's a radio. It's a picture gallery. What is "it"? A computer!

Computers can be all of these things when they're connected to the right multimedia sites on the Web. The word "multimedia" describes all the stuff (in addition to plain text) that comes from computers. The Web is packed with multimedia features, like sound and video, that make using a computer fun for kids.

Multimedia users might start using the TV and radio less and the computer more. Sites like Broadcast.com play CDs and signals from radio stations right through the computer. It's like having a personal jukebox! It takes a couple of special programs to use all this stuff, but each site explains what's needed and where to find it for free.

It only takes a few seconds to look up all kinds of photos at The Amazing Picture Machine. Other sites, such as the ZooNet Image Archives, have pictures of one thing—animals. Add some wild sound effects from a site like SoundAmerica, and the computer becomes a real funhouse of sights and sounds!

See out-of-this-world pictures of scientists, astronauts, and space ships

Galactic Odyssey

http://library.advanced.org/11348/#Video_Gallery

Most of history passed by before anyone could take pictures or movies of it. Photographic cameras hadn't been invented when Egyptians built the pyramids, and there weren't any TV cameras around to film the War of 1812. Fortunately, kids studying space travel don't have that problem. Cameras have taken pictures of all the rockets and astronauts that humans have sent into space. The Galactic Odyssey Web site has put a lot of these photos and movies online. This collection is an awesome way to see the people and machines that have explored space.

The video gallery is loaded with movies. Kids first need to get the QuickTime program (http://www.apple.com/quicktime) in order to watch the films. (The program is free.) The movies cover everything from man's first step on the moon to images of the space shuttle blasting off on a mission. The photos of rockets are a bit fuzzy, but they offer a peek at the machines that carry people away from Earth.

Read the stories behind the pictures; you'll find information on rocketry, pioneers of space travel, and medical advances made through space exploration. There are also pictures of famous scientists, such as Albert Einstein and Isaac Newton.

LINKS:
NASA, Medical Advances, Your Space Prediction

Listen to radio stations from around the world

Broadcast.com

http://www.broadcast.com

Computers become the world's strongest radios when they're tuned into Broadcast.com. This cool site brings in broadcasts of music, sports, and talk shows from around the world. It's a blast listening to a radio station broadcasting live from the other side of the country. It's like taking a trip without leaving the house!

Another feature is the CD jukebox. It's filled with thousands of CDs that users can listen to. What a great way to hear the latest from your favorite band! Most major news and sports events are available through this site as well.

Sites such as Broadcast.com are really on the cutting edge. Soon, people might even trade in their radios for computers! To use Broadcast.com, a computer needs the RealPlayer program. Parents can find it for free at the company's Web site (http://www.real.com).

Special features tune the computer into programs like lectures from educational conferences or audio books (where someone reads stories out loud). There are even live TV channels where kids can watch exciting events (such as the space shuttle blasting off). The picture quality isn't as good as that of a TV, but this feature is still worth checking out.

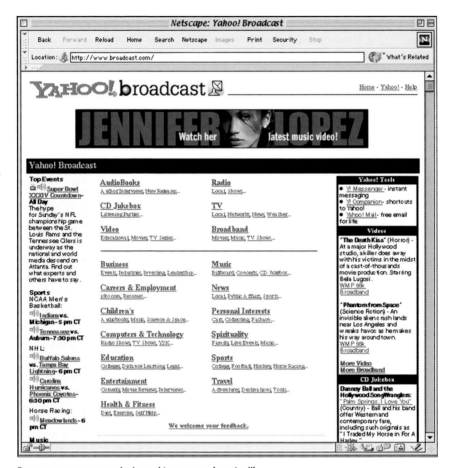

From sports to news to the latest hits, you can hear it all!

LINKS:
NASA TV, CD Jukebox, AudioBooks

Take an online safari and study pictures of wild animals

ZooNet Image Archives

http://www.mindspring.com/~zoonet/gallery.html

Some animal watchers have to crouch in hot, sticky jungles or on cold, windy mountains to get glimpses of wild creatures. Smart Web users know there's a better way to get an up-close look at animals. They just visit the ZooNet Image Archives site for pictures of hundreds of different creatures from around the world. The pictures are great, and nobody has to worry about getting chomped by a polar bear or trampled by a rhinoceros!

Users can find photos of almost any animal by scrolling down the page to the Animal Pictures section. It has links to collections of photos organized by types of animals, such as Birds and Fowl, Carnivores, Monkeys and Apes, and Rodents. Within each section, finding a picture is as easy as clicking an animal's name. Most of these color pictures are very clear, and the fangs on a cougar or the feathers on a swan seem to jump off the screen. There are several different shots available of most animals. For instance, kids can see a giraffe in both walking and resting positions.

LINKS:
Birmingham Zoo Gallery, Jackson Zoo Gallery, Primate Gallery, ZooSpell

Decorate your computer or your wall with great animal photos.

Let your computer do the talking

Sound FX page

http://www.vionline.com/sound.html

If you want to make your computer laugh, cry, sneeze, cough, or even croak, download a few sound files from this page. You'll find sounds in several categories, including animal sounds, bells, and car sounds.

Once you download any of the sounds (they're all pretty small so they won't fill up your computer's hard drive), you can use them in school reports or in a slide show or even make them greet you when you turn on the computer. Wouldn't it be cool to add the sound of a croaking bullfrog to a multimedia report on the rainforest? Or how about just listening to a nice hearty chuckle when you're in a bad mood? You'll find a whole lot of laughs on this page from men, women, and even chipmunks. Once you've saved a sound on your computer, you can listen to it anytime.

Even if you don't want to save any of the sounds to your computer, it's fun to click on the different sound effects, just to hear what they are.

> **Your computer may already have sounds built in. Ask your parents to check by going to the Control Panel and clicking on "sounds." You can see which sounds you have and if there are ones you want to add to an event (like opening a file or logging off the computer).**

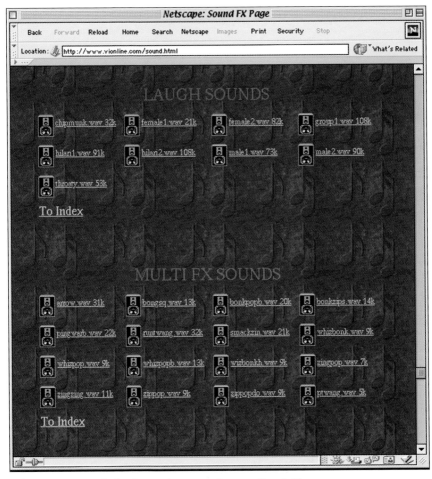

Make your computer the funniest, coolest, or scariest-sounding of all!

Can you guess what a photon sounds like? A whizpop? With more than 100 sound effects on this page, you're sure to find one to liven up your computer.

You'll soon be singin' in the rain

Musical Meteorology

http://www.wxdude.com

Can you tell a cumulus cloud from a cirrus cloud? How do meteorologists predict the weather? What causes thunder and lightning? If your parents don't know the answers to these questions, just tune in to the Weather Dude! Parents and kids alike will enjoy learning all about the weather through these delightful songs written and performed by The Weather Dude, a TV weathercaster originally from Seattle.

For the lowdown on rain, snow, and sleet, listen to "What Makes Rain?" The site has the lyrics to ten songs, and you can listen to a clip from each song. You'll find out that "Air can be so cold, air can be so warm. When both combine together, rainy skies are born." There are also songs on snow, the sun, thunder and lightning, cloud cover, wind, and the seasons. The songs all use simple language to explain what are sometimes complicated concepts, and kids will learn a lot as they sing along with the catchy lyrics.

> Kids fascinated by the weather will find a lot of information at meteorologist Nick Walker's site. Kids can find out how to become a weathercaster, how to make a weather station, and how to hear radio shows about the weather. There's also a page on weather proverbs and what they mean.

If you really like the Weather Dude's songs, he also has written a book with a complete set of lyrics as well as full recordings of all ten songs. The book also has weather-related projects and experiments for kids.

LINKS:
Today's Weather, Favorite Books, Meteorology A-Z, Questions and Quizzes

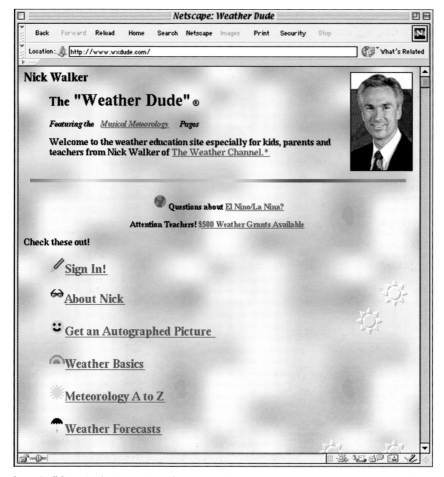

Learn it all from sunrise to sunset—and more.

Listen to wild animals screech and roar–in your own home

Sound Safaris

http://www.wildsanctuary.com/safari.html

Anybody can use a computer to call up animals around the world and hear what they're saying. Well, people can't really "call" animals. But the Sound Safaris Web site lets users hear

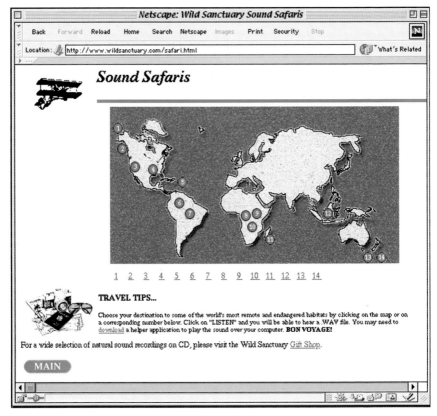

Find out what a cheetah sounds like.

recordings of what all kinds of animals are saying. A few animals are angry, some are looking for friends, and some just want to keep everybody away from their homes.

A map of the world appears on the main page of this Web site. Kids just point to the part of the world they want to visit. Tours head to North America, South America, Africa, and even Antarctica. North America features native animals such as rattlesnakes and walruses. Clicking the Listen button plays a sound clip of a walrus clacking its teeth and a rattlesnake making its scary rattling sound. (Those sounds mean that it's smart to stay away!)

> Every sound that an animal makes is made for a reason. Sometimes animals are trying to attract mates. Sometimes they make sounds to warn their friends of danger or tell them that they've found food.

The text next to each picture explains how and why each animal makes its sound. For instance, a rattlesnake's rattle is made of the same kind of stuff as a person's fingernails; lemurs shriek to tell other lemurs, "Stay off my turf!"; and seals make sounds that can be heard up to 15 miles away underwater. Any kids who still feel wild after visiting this site can check out the Sound Safaris links.

LINKS:
Resources, Antarctic Journal, Gift Shop

A friendly bear shares art with visitors

Billy Bear's Playground

http://www.billybear4kids.com

Billy Bear likes to help kids. So he built this Web site and stuffed it full of cool things kids can use, such as drawings and moving pictures for the computer screen. Billy Bear's pictures are "clip art." That means users can take them off his site and use them for projects or to decorate their computer screen.

Billy lets everyone choose what packages of pictures to take. His regular clip art collections have all kinds of fun drawings of things like butterflies, kids, and cars. He also has packages of drawings for holidays, such as Christmas and Easter.

He has lots of other tools for making computers more interesting, too. Billy Bear's screen savers can really dress up kids' monitors. Screen savers put pictures on the screen after the computer hasn't been used for a while. Then, when someone comes back to use the computer, they might be greeted by a polar bear or baby animal of their choice telling them that they did their best today! Instructions for using the screen savers are on the Web site. Parents can read the instructions and help set up the screen savers.

LINKS:
Animal Scoop, StoryBooks, Show & Tell

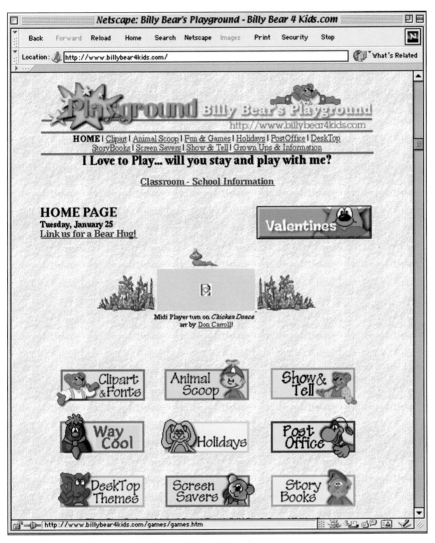

Give your computer a boost with all sorts of fun stuff!

Sufferin' succotash! It's Cartoon World

Cartoon World

http://www.cet.com/~rascal/welcome.html

Cartoons aren't only on TV and in the movies. They're also on the computer screen for the visitors of Cartoon World. This

Say hi to your favorite characters!

super 'toon hangout has sounds, video clips, pictures, and even some games from kids' favorite cartoons.

The World's Greatest link points to some of the all-time favorite characters. Check out the video clips of Simba and Pumba from *The Lion King*. Big stars such as Winnie the Pooh, Marvin the Martian, and the Flintstones have their pictures on this site. You can save these pictures on your computer screen! Look down the page for songs from shows such as *The Jetsons* and *Inspector Gadget*. Click the links and sing along!

Fans of adventure and action cartoons can find goodies here, too. There are sounds and video clips from *Voltron*, *Johnny Quest*, *He-Man*, *Transformers*, and *The Thundercats*. Some cartoons have special features; for instance, the characters from *Scooby Doo* appear on coloring book pages.

One of the best areas at Cartoon World is under the Fun & Games button on the main page. The challenge is to identify cartoon characters just by their shadows.

LINKS:
Starblazers, Saturday Morning Live, Mystery, Action

Get down while learning

Schoolhouse Rock

http://genxtvland.simplenet.com/ SchoolHouseRock/index-lo.shtml

Sometimes it's easier to learn things by singing. The right tune can help kids learn math, history, and even grammar. That's what makes *Schoolhouse Rock* so much fun. These musical cartoons have been playing on Saturday mornings since before most kids were born, and they've helped millions of children learn. Now everybody can watch the cartoons whenever they want, thanks to the *Schoolhouse Rock* Web site.

At the site's main page, visitors pick a subject to learn about: Grammar Rock, Multiplication Rock, America Rock, or Scooter Computer & Mr. Chips. Inside each area, kids can choose an episode of *Schoolhouse Rock* to listen or to watch. Hits here include "Conjunction Junction," "No More Kings," and "Naughty Number Nine." After watching the last one a couple of times, kids will be able to multiply *any* number by nine! Kids will have to load RealAudio and QuickTime on their computers to hear the sounds and watch the cartoons.

There is enough here to keep kids learning for a long time. Check out the story of where *Schoolhouse Rock* came from and the TV listings so you can catch the Rock on TV.

LINKS:
Events, Products, About This Site

There might be a TV inside your computer

SoundAmerica

http://www.soundamerica.com

Surfing the World Wide Web always sounds like fun. But the SoundAmerica Web site helps computers really make some noise with clips from famous cartoons, movies, television shows, and wacky sound effects that make everybody laugh. This is one site that definitely sounds like a good time.

Each section lists the clips available. When users click one, they'll have to wait a few seconds while the clip loads up. Some of the sound effects are gross, like the barfing noise or the big belch. Others are just funny, like mooing cows or the "boing" sound that cartoons use a lot. The Cartoons section has clips from lots of kids' favorite funny characters. There's a clip of Scooby Doo laughing. There's even Elmer Fudd talking about how he'll finally get that "scwewy wabbit."

All of the sound clips are fun to listen to at the site. Plus, kids can download them to their own computers and hear the Tasmanian Devil or Porky Pig whenever they feel like it.

LINKS:
Sound FAQ, Sound Gallery

Follow the White Rabbit with Alice

Alice's Adventures in Wonderland

http://www.megabrands.com/alice/goalice.html

The classic story "Alice in Wonderland" tells of a little girl's adventures in a strange place where cats disappear and rabbits carry watches. By clicking Online Edition, readers can jump into this weird world at the Alice's Adventures in Wonderland site. They can read the book online, but this site has more to offer than just a book. It's full of surprises such as drawings that move (and even talk) when least expected.

Things start, of course, with the first chapter. Pretty music plays as visitors read about how Alice chases a strange white rabbit down a hole. Before long, she falls deep in the hole and winds up looking at a bottle labeled "Drink Me." Did she drink what was in the bottle? Visit the site to find out, and then join her for the rest of her wild adventures.

It's easy to get caught up in the story. Alice talks as she explores Wonderland. And that weird little rabbit even winks and runs away when readers look at the pictures. It's almost like being in Wonderland! There are also other books that kids can download. Kids can also read all about Lewis Carroll, who created Alice and all her friends.

Check out a great fantasy classic!

One word is worth a dozen pictures at this site

The Amazing Picture Machine

http://www.ncrtec.org/picture.htm

The World Wide Web is like the world's largest photo album. It has pictures of everything from aardvarks to zeppelins. The Amazing Picture Machine helps users find the pictures they need in this giant library of photos. Just type the name of a person, place, or thing, and the Picture Machine will point out where to find the pictures. This is the perfect tool for finding pictures for fun or photos to liven up school reports on people, machines, animals, or anything else.

Visitors just type in the name of what they're looking for and click the Start Search button. Searching for "giraffe," for example, brings pictures of giraffes hanging out around trees. Descriptions tell all about each picture, whether it's color or black-and-white, and list some technical stuff, such as how big it is.

A clickable link brings up the picture. When kids find a picture they like, they can click it with their right mouse button and choose Save Picture As to save it on the computer's hard drive. Kids should check each Web site to make sure the pictures' owners don't mind people using them.

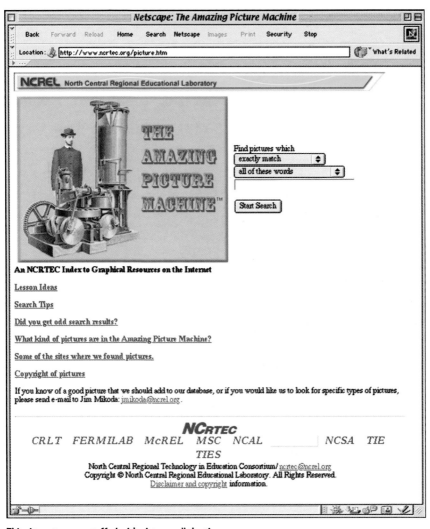

This site gets more stuffed with pictures all the time.

Glossary

Address. The unique location of either (1) an Internet server, (2) a specific file (for example, a Web page), or (3) an e-mail user.

Archive. An electronic attic for storing old information, such as articles from old issues of an online magazine or questions already answered by a homework expert. Many Web sites put out new information all the time, but they save all the old information in an archive.

Binary. Related to a system of numbers having "2" as its base.

Bookmark. A Web browser tool that makes it easy to revisit sites the user likes. Kids, when visiting a site they like, mark it with a bookmark. They then choose the Bookmarks option in their Web browser to see a list of all the sites they've bookmarked. Click one to visit the site. Also called Favorites in some Web browsers.

Browser. Computer software that lets users visit Web sites. Microsoft Internet Explorer and Netscape Navigator are the most popular Web browsers. Browsers are the places where users click buttons, links, and pictures to move around in Web sites.

CD-ROM. A disc that looks just like a music compact disc (CD) but stores computer programs. Almost all software now comes on CD-ROM, and many people call software "CD-ROMs."

Chat. An Internet feature that lets users type messages that appear on a friend's screen as soon as they type them. When several people get together to chat, they're in a "chat room." It's almost like having a real-life conversation, except users read what others say on the screen instead of hearing it.

Clip Art. Pictures people take off the Web to use however they want. Someone who needed a picture of a monkey, for instance, could visit a clip art Web site, and when they found one, they could download it. Clip art gets its name because the pictures used to be on paper, and people "clipped" them out of a book and pasted them onto other papers.

Copyright. A legal rule that says people own what they create. If someone draws a picture, they can copyright it; that means no one else can use that picture without their permission. Users can't use copyrighted pictures, sounds, or movies without permission from the person who created them. Make sure a Web site grants permission for people to use its pictures before downloading them.

Data. Data is information that has been translated into a form that is more convenient to move or process. Relative to today's computers and transmission media, data is information converted either into binary or digital form.

Digital. Related to a system of numbers expressed directly as digits.

Discussion Board. A general term for any online "bulletin board" where you can leave messages and expect to see responses to messages you have posted. Or you can simply read the board. Bulletin board services were invented for this purpose (as well as to allow for the exchange of uploaded/downloaded files). On the Internet, UseNet provides thousands of discussion boards. Chat groups form a kind of real-time discussion board.

Disk. A data storage device. See Floppy disk and Hard disk.

Disk Drive. A device used to retrieve and store data and programs on a disk.

Display. See Monitor.

Download. To take pictures, sounds, programs, or other information off the Internet and put it on the user's computer.

E-mail. An Internet feature that lets people send typed messages to friends. It's like mailing a regular letter, except the message is electronic and travels quickly over the Internet. E-mail can go around the world in less than five minutes! Users can attach files, such as pictures and sound clips, to e-mail messages.

FAQs. Frequently Asked Questions. Lists of FAQs answer the questions people usually have when they first visit a site, such as, "Where did you get the name for this site?" Check out FAQs to figure out what's going on when first arriving at a site.

Floppy Disk. A plastic disk that stores data. Older 5.25-inch disks were housed in a thin, flexible casing, hence the name "floppy." Today's 3.5-inch disks and Zip disks are housed in hard plastic.

Hard Disk, Hard Drive. A large-capacity storage device used for quick retrieval and storage of computer data. All computers manufactured now have hard drives built in. Application software and user-created files are stored on the hard disk.

Home Page. The main page for a Web site.

HTML. HyperText Markup Language. The programming language used to create Web pages. A lot of programs now exist that use HTML to make creating Web pages easier.

HTTP. HyperText Transfer Protocol. The Internet standard that supports the exchange of information on the Web.

Hyperlink. Words on a Web site that users can click to visit another Web page. Hyperlinks (called "links" for short) are usually underlined and appear in a different color.

Interactive. A Web site or computer program that lets the user enter information or control what happens on the screen. One kind of interactive Web site might let someone solve a puzzle by moving blocks around the screen with their mouse.

Internet. A network that connects computers around the world. When a computer is connected to the Internet, that computer's user can access stories, pictures, sounds, movies, and all kinds of other information other Internet users have put out there for them to see. It's like exploring new places, except the information travels over telephone lines and through a computer.

ISP. Internet Service Provider. A company that has its own bank of computers and phone lines to allow users to dial into the Internet.

Java. A special programming language that runs little programs on Web pages. Sometimes the games kids play at a Web site use Java.

Keyboard. On most computers, the primary text input device. It contains certain standard function keys, such as Escape, tab, cursor movement keys, shift and control keys, and, sometimes, other manufacturer-customized keys.

Log-on, Log-in. The procedure used to get access to an operating system or application, usually in a remote computer. A log-on almost always requires a user to have (1) a user ID and (2) a password.

Memory. Data storage capacity, usually measured in kilobytes (KB) or megabytes (MB).

Modem. A part inside (or sometimes outside) the computer that lets the computer connect to a telephone line and talk with other computers around the world. A computer using a modem is making a phone call just like people do, except its conversations bring up Web pages and transfer e-mail instead of spoken conversations.

Monitor. The TV-like screen driven by a computer's video card. Also called a display.

Mouse. A handheld tool used to point to things on a computer screen. Point the arrow on the screen to something and click the mouse button by pressing and releasing it. Some mouses have a right-hand button that provides more functions.

Multimedia. Any kind of information on the computer screen other than plain words. Multimedia includes pictures, sounds, and movies.

Netscape. The short form of "Netscape Navigator," Netscape is the most widely used World Wide Web browser or user interface.

Operating System. Software that controls the computer by performing basic tasks, such as organizing memory and facilitating communication between components; for example, Windows and Mac OS.

Password. A secret word people use to get into Web sites that only let their members in. When users join some Web clubs, they will get to make up a password and then use it every time they visit the Web site.

PC (Personal Computer). A computer designed for use by one person at a time. Also used to describe an "IBM-compatible" personal computer, as opposed to an Apple Macintosh. The PC is associated with business as well as home use.

Pixels. Picture elements. The dots that combine to form images on a monitor.

Printer. A device that accepts information (such as text and pictures) from a computer and puts it onto paper.

QuickTime. A program users can add to their Web browser in order to watch recorded films online. QuickTime can be downloaded for free, and it's easy to add to the browser.

RAM. Random access memory. Temporary memory that stores data while a computer is on. Usually referred to in KB or MB.

RealAudio. A special program users can add to their Web browser in order to listen to recorded sounds and music online. RealAudio lets users try out songs on CDs they're thinking of buying or hear sound clips from their favorite movies.

RealAudio can be downloaded for free, and it's easy to add to the browser.

RealPlayer. This is just like RealAudio, except it also lets users watch movies online.

Resolution. The detail and sharpness of an image as presented on a monitor or printed page. The higher the resolution, the sharper the image.

ROM. Read-only memory. Data that is stored in ROM is permanent, unlike RAM, which requires electrical current to maintain data.

Scanner. A device that turns regular pictures and printed stuff into information on a computer screen. It is kind of like a photocopier, but instead of making copies, it makes electronic images of the original.

Screen Saver. A picture that comes up on a computer screen if the user hasn't used the computer for a while. Screen savers got their name because old monitors could be damaged if one image stayed on the screen too long. Screen savers put changing pictures up that "saved" the screen from damage. Now screen savers are just for fun, and a lot of them are available on the Internet for kids to download for free.

Search Engine. A Web site that helps users find information online. People can go to a search engine, such as Yahooligans!, and type in the words "Bugs Bunny" to get a list of all the sites out there with information on that cartoon. A search engine is like the card catalog at the library; it is the best place to start looking for information.

Shockwave. A special program users can add to their Web browser so they can view animations such as cartoons and play lots of games. When a site has features that require Shockwave, a message will let you know. Users can download Shockwave for free.

Site. The name for a collection of Web pages on one topic put up by one person or group.

Surfing. The word for cruising around the Internet, looking for information.

URL. Uniform Resource Locator. The fancy name for a Web page's address. Things like "http://www.nickelodeon.com" are URLs.

User. Computer user. This is the name for people when they are "using" their computers.

Video Card. The card that drives and controls the computer's video display.

Virtual. A word that describes Internet versions of things found in real life. A virtual postcard isn't a real postcard you drop in the mail; it's an electronic message that people can send. A virtual zoo may be an online collection of pictures of animals in a real zoo somewhere.

Virus. A piece of programming code put into another program to cause some unexpected and, for the recipient, usually undesirable event. Viruses can be transmitted by downloading programming from other sites, or they may be present on a floppy disk.

World Wide Web. The easy-to-use part of the Internet that includes pictures and lots of buttons people can click. Most of the time users are online, they'll be working with the Web.

Yahoo! One of the most famous and easiest to use Web search engines. Yahoo! is a free service and lets users type in words to search for on the Web. It also organizes sites into categories such as "Travel" and "Music."

Index

My Favorite Web Sites
and Addresses